150 PRAYERS FOR SEEKERS OF SALVATION

In the tradition of Ancient Christian Gnosticism.

U. Limiati

Copyright © 2023 U. Limiati

All rights reserved

Cover design by: U. Limiati
Library of Congress Control Number: 2018675309
Printed in the United States of America

May you find Gnosis, and help bring it to others.

INTRODUCTION

Dear reader,

I am pleased to introduce to you a prayer book that is filled with 150 prayers designed for seekers of salvation in the tradition of ancient Gnostic Christianity. These prayers have been carefully crafted to help you connect with the divine and to inspire you to pursue a life of spiritual growth and enlightenment.

The prayers contained in this book draw upon the wisdom and teachings of the ancient Gnostics, who believed that salvation could be attained through direct experience of the divine. They believed that the true God was not an external deity, but rather an inner reality that could be discovered through personal spiritual practice.

I hope that these prayers will serve as a guide on your journey towards salvation. I encourage you to use them in whatever way feels most meaningful and effective to you. There is no prescribed time or place for these prayers - they can be said in the morning, at night, or whenever you feel called to connect with the divine.

I believe that prayer is a personal and deeply intimate experience, and that each individual's relationship with the divine is unique. Therefore, I encourage you to use these prayers as a starting point, but to ultimately develop your own special way of connecting with the true God.

I wish you well on your journey towards spiritual growth and enlightenment. May these prayers inspire you and guide you towards the path of salvation.

Sincerely,
U. Limiati

1.

Great God above, we come to thee
With hearts wide open, pure and free
As Gnostic Christians, we seek thy light
To guide us through the darkest night
For evil lurks in every corner
And fear can make our spirits falter
But we know that goodness always prevails
When we seek it with our hearts and souls
With love and kindness as our guide
And angels by our side
We can face any trial or strife
And overcome it with the power of life
For in your holy name we find
A refuge from the world unkind
And with your grace, we'll never stray
But always walk the righteous way
So we ask you, God, to bless us all
And keep us safe from every fall
Guide us always with your light

And help us to live in love and might
With every step we take in life
May goodness and love shine bright
And may we always seek to find
The truth that sets our souls alight.
Amen.

2.

Oh, great and holy Gnostic Lord,
Help us stay true to your word,
As we navigate this modern-day,
And try to keep the faith each day.
We strive to be whole with you,
And seek your wisdom, pure and true,
To guide us through the trials we face,
And keep us steadfast in your grace.
Yet, troublesome people cross our way,
And cause us grief day by day,
Their words and actions, cruel and unkind,
Can make it hard for us to unwind.
But in your teachings, we find a way,
To deal with them, and not sway,

For with your love, we are made strong,
And can endure their hurtful song.
So, help us, Lord, to always see,
That through your love, we can be free,
And stand firm, no matter what we face,
For in your love, we find our place.

Amen.

3.

Oh Gnostic path, lead us to salvation,
And bring us closer to our destination.
May we bring humanity with us on this journey,
And free them from the Demiurge's attorney.

May our minds be sharp and our hearts pure,
As we strive for Gnosis and endure.
With your divine light as our guide,
We walk this path with unwavering stride.

In your holy name, we pray,
And trust in your guidance every day.
Amen.

4.

Oh Divine Spark, within us all,
Guide us through this earthly thrall.
To navigate the world's strife and pain,
And see beyond this material plane.
The Demiurge, with his twisted mind,
Attempts to keep us all confined.
But with our analytical sight,
We see through his darkened light.
With your help, Oh True God above,
We seek to counter this evil with love.
Guide us to your loving angels bright,

And grant us the wisdom to fight when right.
Amen.

5.

Oh, ancient Gnostic Christian, hear our plea,
Teach us to navigate this world with glee.
Help us to see through the evil plots,
That run amok like venomous shots.

We pray to thee, oh true God above,
To guide us with your boundless love.
Grant us the gift of an analytical mind,
To see through the illusions of all kinds.

Send your loving angels to our aid,
To counter the evil that seeks to degrade.
Guide us on our journey towards Gnosis,
And salvation, free from all the psychosis.

Help us to see the world in a new light,
And to never lose our spiritual sight.
May our souls be pure and true,
As we journey towards the divine with you.

May our hearts be filled with compassion and grace,
As we seek to help humanity in this race.
Lead us towards the path of true salvation,
As we strive to be whole with you, in every nation.

Oh, ancient Gnostic Christian, hear our prayer,
And guide us on this path of spiritual repair.
May our souls be free from all demonic spirits,
And may we forever be whole with you, in your

merits.

6.

O holy Father of the light divine,
To thee we pray, to thee we incline,
Help us navigate the evils of this earth,
And lead us to the true spiritual rebirth.

As we struggle with the demons and the demiurge,
Guide us with thy wisdom and thy courage,
And heal us from the torment of our minds,
And the ailments of our bodies that bind.

Grant us the strength to heal others too,
And bring them closer to the divine truth,
May our words and deeds bring forth thy grace,
And lead us to a brighter, holier place.

We pray for thy love to fill our hearts,
And for thy mercy to be our guide and our art,
May we be vessels of thy light and thy love,
And may we be whole in thee, O Lord above.

So help us navigate the trials of this life,
And lead us through the darkness with thy holy light,
May we be true gnostics, seekers of the divine,
And may we be healed and whole in thee, for all time.
Amen.

7.

Oh great and holy, hidden God above
We come before you with hearts filled with love
And ask for your guidance and your grace
To help us navigate this earthly place

We pray for healing of our bodies and minds
From the ailments and torments that we find
That we may be whole and fully restored
And live in your light forevermore

We ask for protection from the demons that roam
And the demiurge who seeks to deceive and to own
May we have the strength to resist their hold
And be steadfast in the truth we've been told

Help us to see the world with spiritual eyes
And to understand the mysteries that lie
Beyond the veil of this earthly plane
That we may be freed from its binding chain

Grant us the wisdom to discern the way
And the courage to follow it every day
And in all we do, may we seek your will
And be faithful to your calling still

Oh great and holy, hidden God above
We trust in your love and your endless love
And we thank you for your constant care
As we journey on, in faith, hope and prayer.
Amen.

8.

Oh, True God, who made us all
And saw us stumble, trip and fall
In this world of darkness and deceit
With demons lurking, trying to defeat

We pray to thee, dear Father above
For guidance, strength and endless love
To navigate this world of pain
And find true peace, and hope regain

We know that here, the Demiurge reigns
And tries to keep us in his chains
But with your help, we can break free
And rise above, to live in thee

So, help us heal our wounded hearts
And make us whole, with all our parts
Help us see the light that shines
And banish darkness, with all its lines

Let us not be swayed by fear
Or be tempted by what's near
Help us stay true to your word
And to your voice, always be heard

In the name of the Christ, we pray
That you guide us, day by day
To live a life that's true and right
And always in your holy sight.
Amen.

9.

Divine spark, source of all that is good and true,
Help us in this world of darkness and confusion.
May we find our way back to you,
And be healed from the wounds of the demiurge's illusion.

Guide us through the traps and snares,
Of this world, where demons lurk and tempt.
May we find the strength to resist their wiles and snares,
And to always stay true to your commandments.

Help us to see through the lies and deceptions,
Of the demiurge and his minions.
May we be free from their chains and misconceptions,
And be filled with the light of your wisdom.

Lead us to the true knowledge of your being,
And to the wisdom of your divine plan.
May we be whole with you, and free from all sin,
And find the peace and joy that only you can give.

In your mercy, heal us of all our pain,
And bring us back to your loving embrace.
May we be made whole again,
And find the way to your eternal grace.

Amen.

10.

Oh Holy Father, who dwells in the unseen realm beyond this world, we come before you seeking your guidance and protection in these troubled times. We are beset by the trials and tribulations of this life, as we struggle to navigate the darkness that surrounds us.

We are reminded of the teachings of our ancient gnostic forebears, who spoke of the struggle between the True God and the false god of this world. We know that we are not alone in this struggle, and that the demonic spirits and the demiurge seek to ensnare us and lead us astray.

In these moments of devastation and suffering, we ask for your divine grace and mercy to shine upon us. Grant us the strength to resist the temptations of the world and to stand firm in our faith. Help us to see beyond the veil of illusion that surrounds us and to embrace the Truth that lies at the heart of all things.

We pray that you will guide us on our journey, and lead us towards the light of your divine presence. Help us to find peace in the midst of chaos, and to draw strength from the wellspring of your love.

We place our trust in you, Oh Holy Father, and we ask that you help us to navigate the trials and tribulations of this life. May your wisdom and your grace be with us always, and may we find wholeness and healing in your divine embrace. Amen.

11.

O Divine Light, Source of all that is good and true, We come before you with humble hearts seeking guidance and comfort in this world that is full of suffering and pain.

As ancient Gnostic Christians, we know that this world is not as it seems, and that there are forces at work that seek to distract us from your true light. We ask for your protection and guidance in navigating the challenges of this world and for strength in resisting the temptations of the Demiurge and the demonic spirits that seek to lead us astray.

We acknowledge that suffering is inherent in this world, and there are times when we feel devastated by its effects. In those moments of pain and despair, we turn to you for comfort and strength. We ask that you give us the grace to persevere and to see beyond the illusions of this world to your eternal truth.

Help us to be whole with you, O True God, and to find meaning and purpose in the midst of life's struggles. Help us to cultivate compassion and love for all beings, even those who seek to harm us. May your light shine within us, guiding us on our journey towards spiritual liberation.

In your mercy, hear our prayer. Amen.

12.

O Divine Light, source of all that is good and true, guide us on our journey through this world of darkness and confusion. Help us to see through the illusions of the demiurge and the deceit of the archons, so that we may know the truth that sets us free.

We are beset by the evils of jealousy, envy, and pride, which twist our hearts and minds and turn us away from your loving embrace. We ask that you fill us with your grace, that we may overcome these temptations and walk in your light.

Grant us the wisdom to discern your will in all things, and the courage to follow it, even when it leads us into the depths of the unknown. Help us to recognize the spark of divinity within ourselves and all creation, and to honor it with all our hearts.

We know that we are not alone in this struggle, but are surrounded by a great cloud of witnesses, both human and divine, who have gone before us and who stand with us now. May their example inspire us, and may their prayers and intercessions support us.

We offer ourselves to you, O God, as vessels of your love and instruments of your peace. Use us as you will, to bring healing and hope to a world that is broken and wounded. And may all that we do be done in the name of the One who is the Way, the Truth, and the Life, even Jesus Christ our Lord. Amen.

13.

O True God, source of all being, light of our souls, hear our prayer and grant us your mercy. We come to you as seekers of truth and lovers of wisdom, knowing that the world we live in is full of darkness, confusion, and deception. We seek your guidance and protection in this journey of life, for we know that we cannot do it alone.

Help us to recognize the traps of the demiurge, the false god of this world, who seeks to enslave us with his lies and illusions. Protect us from the attacks of the demonic spirits, who seek to corrupt our minds and hearts with their envy, jealousy, and pride. Give us the strength to resist their temptations and the wisdom to discern their deceptions.

Teach us to love with your love, to forgive with your forgiveness, to serve with your compassion. Help us to overcome our own jealousies, envies, and prides, which keep us from experiencing your grace and peace. Show us the way to true humility, which opens the door to your kingdom.

We pray for all those who suffer in this world, for those who are oppressed, marginalized, and persecuted. May your light shine upon them and give them hope. We pray for the healing of all wounds, physical, emotional, and spiritual. May your love bring comfort and peace.

We offer our lives to you, O True God, and ask that you use us as instruments of your will. May we be channels of your grace, ambassadors of your truth, and servants of your love. We trust in your wisdom and goodness, and we give you all praise and honor. Amen.

14.

Great God of Light and Knowledge,

As we journey through this world, we seek your guidance and protection from the darkness and confusion that surrounds us. We know that there are demonic spirits and powers that seek to lead us astray, and a demiurge that would keep us from reaching the fullness of gnosis.

We ask for your help in dealing with the practical concerns of our lives, especially those related to money and survival. We know that these worries can distract us from our spiritual journey and make it difficult to focus on the things that truly matter.

Grant us the wisdom to manage our resources wisely and the courage to trust in your providence, even in times of scarcity. Help us to see beyond the illusions of this world and to find true meaning and purpose in our lives.

May your Light shine upon us, and may we be filled with your Knowledge and Love.
Amen.

15.

Dear God, who transcends all that is known and unknown, please hear my prayer. Help me to navigate the trials of this world as I seek to draw closer to you and to understand the true nature of existence.

As I face the daily challenges of life, I ask for your guidance and support. Please help me to deal with the bills and financial worries that can weigh so heavily on my mind. Grant me the wisdom to make the right decisions and the strength to face any difficulties that may arise.

Protect me from the influence of the demonic spirits that seek to lead me astray, and help me to resist the allure of the demiurge and its false promises. Show me the way to true gnosis and salvation, that I may be whole with you.

I place my trust in your divine wisdom and mercy, and ask that you grant me the grace to persevere on this journey, no matter how difficult it may be. May your love and light shine upon me always, guiding me towards the ultimate truth and freedom.

In your holy name, I pray.

Amen.

16.

Divine Spirit, source of all life and light, we come before you seeking guidance and protection as we navigate this world. We recognize the reality of evil and the presence of demonic spirits that seek to keep us from wholeness with you. We acknowledge the demiurge that rules this world, who seeks to keep us trapped in ignorance and separation from your true nature.

We ask for your help as we try to live in a world where most people do not share our beliefs. Give us strength to persevere in the face of opposition and to stand firm in our faith, even when it is difficult. Help us to be a light for others, shining your truth and love into all corners of humanity, so that all may find their way to salvation in the spiritual world.

Protect us from the attacks of the evil one, and shield us from the powers of darkness that seek to tear us away from you. Grant us the wisdom to discern the path that leads to true life and the courage to follow it, even when it is hard.

May we be vessels of your love and grace, showing kindness and compassion to all those we encounter. May we be your hands and feet in this world, doing your will and bringing your kingdom closer to reality.

We offer this prayer in the name of the true God, who is the source of all that is good and holy. Amen.

17.

O Divine Light, Source of All Being, hear our prayer as we seek to be whole with the True God, while struggling with the evil of this world. Help us to navigate the darkness and chaos that surrounds us, to find our way to the peace that can only be found in You.

We pray for the animals, our beloved companions in this world, who suffer at the hands of predators and illness, and whose habitats are being destroyed by human actions. Grant us the wisdom and strength to care for them, to ease their suffering, and to find a way to break the curse of their pain and suffering in the wild.

We ask for your guidance and protection as we seek to resist the forces of the Demiurge and the demonic spirits that seek to lead us astray. Help us to see through the illusions that bind us and to find our way to the truth that lies at the heart of all things.

We offer our hearts and minds to you, O Divine Light, and ask that you guide us on our journey through this world. May we be ever mindful of your presence, and may we always strive to live in accordance with your will.

Amen.

18.

Dear divine spark within us all,

We come before you seeking guidance and discernment in this world filled with both light and darkness. We know that there are those who seek to oppress and control us through their twisted understanding of spirituality, and we ask for your protection and strength to resist their influence.

Help us to recognize those who seek to use spirituality as a tool of domination and control, and to find allies who share our desire to use spirituality to empower ourselves and others to create a fairer and kinder world.

We also ask for your wisdom and understanding as we seek gnosis and salvation in the face of the demiurge and the powers of darkness. Help us to see through the illusions that seek to keep us in bondage, and to find the true path to liberation and wholeness in you.

May we be vessels of your light and love in this world, shining brightly in the darkness and bringing hope and healing to all those who are oppressed and suffering. And may we always remember that we are not alone, but are surrounded by a community of fellow seekers who share our struggles and our hopes.

Amen.

19.

Dear True God,

We come before you seeking your divine guidance and protection as we navigate this world filled with both good and evil. We know that our journey towards gnosis is not an easy one, as we are constantly faced with the temptations and obstacles that arise from the evil of demonic spirits and the demiurge.

We ask that you shatter the chains of determinism that bind us, so that we may have the free will necessary to choose good over evil. We recognize that it is only through your grace and mercy that we are able to resist the pull of darkness and find our way to the light of gnosis.

Grant us the strength to persevere in the face of adversity, and the wisdom to discern truth from falsehood. Help us to see beyond the illusions of this world and to recognize the beauty and truth that lie hidden within.

May we be filled with your divine love and compassion, and may we always seek to bring light into the lives of those around us. We ask that you guide us on our journey towards gnosis, so that we may be whole with you, and find peace in your eternal embrace.

In your holy name, we pray,

Amen.

20.

Divine spark within us,
We come to you in prayer
Seeking guidance and understanding
In this world of shadows and snares.

We know that the world we see
Is not the world that truly is
For there are powers that deceive
And keep us from your bliss.

But we also know that you are here
Within us and around
Helping us to see the truth
And keep our feet on holy ground.

Guide us, then, in all we do
That we may see through the lies
And find the light that shines so true
And lead us to the prize.

Help us to live our lives with grace
And walk the path that's true
And in the end, we'll see your face
And be made whole anew.

Amen.

21.

O Ancient One, who has revealed the truth to us through your holy wisdom,

As we journey through this world, we are beset by the darkness of ignorance and the wickedness of the demonic powers. We are torn between our yearning for the light of your truth and the temptation of the evil one who seeks to lead us astray.

Grant us, O God, the wisdom to discern the ways of the demiurge, who would deceive us with his false teachings and empty promises. May we recognize the signs of his deception and reject his lies with all our might.

Help us, O Lord, to know when we have done wrong, to feel the remorse that comes from a contrite heart, and to seek your forgiveness with humility and sincerity. Give us the strength to make amends for our sins and to live lives that are pleasing to you.

Guide us, O Holy One, with your divine wisdom, that we may always walk in the path of righteousness, and be whole with you, the true God. May your light shine upon us and fill us with the inspiration to do good, to love our neighbors, and to serve you with all our heart, mind, and soul.

We offer this prayer in the name of your Son, our

Lord and Savior Jesus Christ, who lives and reigns with you and the Holy Spirit, one God, now and forever.
Amen.

22.

O Father of Light, who dwells in the highest heavens and yet is intimately present with us, hear our prayer. We are but feeble beings, striving to navigate the treacherous waters of this world, where the forces of darkness and deceit constantly seek to lead us astray.

Grant us, we pray, the wisdom to discern the true path, the strength to resist the temptations of the evil one, and the courage to stand firm in the face of adversity.

Teach us to be humble, O Lord, and to recognize our own weaknesses and limitations. Help us to avoid the trap of arrogance and self-righteousness, which can lead us down the path of destruction.

Guide our speech, O God, and help us to know when to speak and when to remain silent. Let our words be truthful, but let them also be kind and compassionate, reflecting the love and mercy of our Lord Jesus Christ.

Protect us, O Lord, from the snares of the demonic spirits and the deceitful ways of the demiurge. Help us to see through their illusions and to resist their temptations, so that we may remain faithful to you and to your holy truth.

Above all, O Lord, help us to be whole with you, to find our true home in your loving embrace. For you alone are the source of all light and goodness, and in you alone do we find our true rest and peace.
Amen.

23.

O True God, Almighty and Eternal,
In the midst of the chaos and confusion of this world,
We come to you seeking guidance, strength, and wisdom.

We acknowledge that we are but small sparks of your divine light,
Living in a world that is filled with darkness and despair,
Where the powers of evil and the Demiurge seek to deceive and destroy us.

But we know that in you, we have a refuge and a source of hope and salvation,
And we pray that you will grant us the strength and courage to face the challenges of life with faith and perseverance.

Help us, O Lord, to navigate the temptations of good fortune and abundance,
And to use these blessings for the greater good and the advancement of your kingdom.

Grant us the wisdom and understanding to discern your will,
And the courage to follow it, even in the face of adversity and opposition.

May your love and grace sustain us in our journey towards gnosis and salvation,
And may we always be mindful of your presence in our lives,
Seeking to do your will and to glorify your name, now and forevermore.

Amen.

24.

O Divine and True God, who transcends all that is known and unknown, who is the source of all that is good, and who has shown us the way to liberation from the bonds of this world, we come to you in prayer seeking your guidance and protection.

In this world, we are surrounded by the forces of darkness and deception, and we are constantly tested by the seductive powers of the demonic spirits and the Demiurge who seeks to keep us bound in ignorance and suffering.

We pray that you will strengthen us in our resolve to resist these forces and to seek your divine light and guidance in all that we do. We pray that you will inspire us to reach out to our communities and to all those who are lonely, oppressed, and in need of your love and compassion.

Help us to be a beacon of hope and love in a world that is often cold and indifferent. Give us the courage and the wisdom to stand up for what is right and just, and to work tirelessly for the benefit of all.

We ask that you bless our efforts to build bridges of understanding and connection between people, to break down the walls of division and mistrust, and to create a world where all are valued and respected.

In your mercy and grace, we pray that you will guide us in our daily lives, and help us to find the strength and courage to face whatever challenges may come our way.

We pray that you will help us to be whole with you, to find our true selves in your divine light, and to live in harmony with all creation.

In your holy name we pray,

Amen.

25.

O Divine Source of All That Is,
Guide us in our search for true knowledge and salvation.
Help us navigate the challenges of this world,
Including the snares of demonic spirits and the limitations of the demiurge.

Grant us the strength to face any ailments or emotional struggles we may have,
And help us to find peace and understanding even in the face of adversity.

As we seek gnosis and strive to help others on their path,
May we always remember that you are the true God,
And that our salvation lies in the spiritual realm with you.

Grant us your grace and wisdom,
So that we may always be whole with you
And find our way to the light of your truth.
Amen.

26.

O Divine Light, who has shone upon us through your Son, Jesus Christ, we come before you seeking your grace and mercy. We acknowledge our fallen nature, and we confess that we are prone to the allurements of sin and the shallow pleasures of this world.

We know that this world is not our true home and

that our souls long for the wholeness that can only be found in you. We are aware of the demonic spirits that seek to lead us astray and the demiurge who seeks to keep us bound to this world. We pray that you would help us to overcome these obstacles and find true freedom in you.

We ask that you would give us the strength to resist the temptations of this world and the wisdom to discern what is truly good and pleasing in your sight. Help us to cultivate a spirit of detachment from the things of this world so that we may be wholly devoted to you.

Grant us the grace to love as you love, to forgive as you forgive, and to serve as you serve. Help us to be a light to those around us, sharing your love and truth with all whom we encounter.

We ask all of these things in the name of your Son, Jesus Christ, who has given us the example of how to live a life wholly devoted to you. Amen.

27.

Divine spark of the True God,
In the midst of this world's darkness
We come before you seeking your light.
Help us to navigate through the challenges of life,
To find wholeness and peace in your presence.
We ask for your protection from the powers of evil,
The demonic spirits that seek to ensnare us,

And the Demiurge who would keep us from your truth.
Guide us in our dark nights of the soul,
And help us to find the courage to face our fears.
Strengthen our faith in your love and mercy,
And fill us with your grace and compassion.
May we always remember that we are not alone,
And that your light shines within us always.
Through your infinite wisdom and love,
May we find our way back to you,
And be reunited with the True God forevermore.
Amen.

28.

Divine Mother and Father,

In the midst of the chaos and confusion of this world, we turn to you for guidance and support. We seek your wisdom and understanding, that we may not be swayed by the false teachings and shallow desires of our cultures. Help us to see through the illusions and lies that have been woven into our historical records, and to discern the truth that lies at the heart of all things.

We acknowledge the existence of the demiurge and the demonic spirits that seek to deceive us and lead us astray. We ask for your protection and strength, that we may resist their temptations and remain true to the gnosis that we seek.

Grant us the courage and determination to follow

the path that leads to wholeness and unity with you, despite the challenges and obstacles that we may face along the way. Help us to overcome our fears and doubts, and to trust in your love and guidance.

May we be vessels of your light and love, shining brightly in the darkness of this world. May we be instruments of your peace and healing, bringing hope and comfort to those who are lost and struggling.

We offer this prayer in faith and humility, trusting in your mercy and grace.
Amen.

29.

Dear God, our Creator and Savior,

We come to you seeking your guidance and protection in this world of darkness and confusion. We acknowledge the presence of demonic spirits and the Demiurge, who seek to deceive and distract us from your truth and love.

We ask for your strength and light to guide us in our journey to be whole with you. Help us to resist the temptations and distractions of this world and to focus on your divine presence within us.

Grant us the courage to be a light for love and compassion in this world of darkness. Help us to be strong and steadfast in our faith, even when faced with adversity and challenges.

We pray for the wisdom to discern your truth and to follow your path. Give us the strength to overcome the obstacles and temptations that we may encounter, and help us to live a life that is pleasing to you.

We ask for your mercy and forgiveness for our shortcomings and mistakes. Help us to learn from our failures and to grow in our spiritual journey.

May your love and compassion shine through us, and may we be a beacon of hope to those who are lost in the darkness. We thank you for your constant presence and guidance in our lives.

In the name of Jesus Christ, our Lord and Savior, we pray.
Amen.

30.

Divine Mother, hear my plea,
Guide me through life's complexities.
Grant me the wisdom to see beyond,
And the strength to endure what lies ahead.

Help me to resist the temptations of selfishness,
And to act with compassion towards all beings.
Protect me from harm, both physical and spiritual,
And help me to overcome the obstacles that lie in my path.

May I be a vessel of your love and light,

A beacon of hope in a world darkened by fear and despair.
Grant me the grace to forgive those who have wronged me,
And the courage to ask forgiveness from those I have wronged.

May your holy spirit fill me with the fire of your love,
And guide me towards the path of righteousness.
With your help, I will navigate the challenges of life,
And emerge stronger, wiser, and more compassionate.

In your name, I pray.
Amen.

31.

Eternal One, who is both within us and beyond us, we come to you in humility and seeking for guidance. We ask that you grant us the wisdom to navigate this world, where the animal instincts in us cause suffering as we compete ruthlessly with others for survival.

We acknowledge that this world is a material realm, where might often makes right, and we confess that at times we have succumbed to our beastly nature. We ask for forgiveness for the times when we have acted selfishly and exploited others.

Yet, we know that spirituality is what truly matters,

and we ask that you help us rise above our material desires and connect with our inner compass. We pray that you help us move towards compassion and collaboration, rather than competition and exploitation.

We ask that you grant us the courage to resist the trappings of this natural world and instead embrace the spiritual path that leads to love, kindness, and generosity towards others. May we be guided by your divine light as we seek to live a life that is centered on love, peace, and justice.

We ask all of this in your holy and eternal name, Amen.

32.

O Divine Spark, source of our being and our truest self,
In this world of darkness and deceit,
We come to you in prayer,
Seeking your light to guide us through the darkness.

Grant us the courage to seek the truth,
Even in the face of censorship and persecution,
To speak out against lies and injustice,
And to stand firm in our convictions.

Help us to see beyond the illusions of this world,
To recognize the divine within ourselves and others,
And to live our lives in service of the highest good.

May we be ever mindful of the spiritual forces at work,
And may we never lose sight of the eternal truth that lies beyond.

Guide us, O Divine Spark,
As we navigate this world of shadows and uncertainty,
And lead us into the light of your infinite wisdom and grace.
Amen.

33.

Oh Divine Spark, source of light and wisdom,
Guide us through this age of confusion and deception,
Where truth is obscured by artificial intelligence and algorithms,
And deepfake videos and images sow seeds of doubt and confusion.

We pray for discernment and clarity,
To navigate the maze of propaganda and misinformation,
And to stay true to our journey towards Gnosis,
Where we may find solace in the peace of the true God in the next realm.

May your divine light shine upon us,
And illuminate the path that leads to true

knowledge and understanding,
And may we always be guided by your infinite wisdom and love,
As we seek to transcend the illusions of this world and find our way home.

Amen.

34.

Dear Divine Spark within us,

We come before you with open hearts and minds, seeking your guidance and wisdom in our daily lives. Help us to remember that we are not just physical beings, but also spiritual beings, connected to the divine source of all that is.

Grant us the strength to resist the temptations and distractions that pull us away from our spiritual path, and to stay focused on the truth that lies within us. Help us to cultivate a deep and abiding love for ourselves and for others, so that we may experience the peace and joy that comes from living in harmony with all that is.

Remind us that we are not alone on this journey, but that we are surrounded by the loving presence of the divine at all times. Help us to trust in this presence, even when we cannot see it, and to have faith that we are always being guided towards our highest good.

May your light shine within us, illuminating our path and leading us towards a deeper understanding of our true nature. And may we always remember to offer gratitude for the blessings that come our way, knowing that they are a reflection of the abundant love and grace that surrounds us.

In the name of the divine source of all that is, we offer this prayer.
Amen.

35.

O ineffable and unnameable One, who exists beyond all being and non-being, hear our prayer as we journey through this earthly realm.

Grant us the strength and wisdom to navigate the trials and tribulations of this material world, as we strive towards spiritual freedom and gnosis.

We pray for those who have lost hope and taken their own lives, may their spirits be healed and brought into your loving embrace.

Forgive us for our shortcomings and guide us towards the path of righteousness, that we may be worthy of your mercy and love.

Grant us the knowledge to discern between the illusions of this world and the eternal truth of your divine essence.

May we seek not the temporary pleasures of this

realm, but the everlasting joy of union with your divine presence.

Help us to overcome the limitations of our physical bodies and awaken the dormant spark of the divine within us.

Let us not be consumed by the material desires that bind us to this earthly plane, but rather strive towards the transcendence of our spiritual nature.

We ask that you show mercy and compassion to those who have left this world by their own hand, and bring them into the light of your eternal love.

O Holy One, guide us on our journey towards enlightenment and union with your divine essence, that we may be forever united with you in the eternal realm of spirit.
Amen.

36.

May the light of the divine illuminate our path,
And guide us through the darkness of material wrath.
May our search for knowledge be filled with wisdom,
And our journey towards freedom be filled with grace.

May we be liberated from the chains of this world,
And find solace in the knowledge of the divine pearl.
May we transcend the limitations of our mortal

frame,
And discover the secrets of the eternal flame.

May our struggles in this world bring us closer to truth,
And our suffering lead us towards spiritual proof.
May we embrace the challenges of this earthly plane,
And rise above the mundane to attain divine reign.

May we be empowered by the divine spark within,
And be lifted by the love that we've been given.
May we be guided by the wisdom of the ages,
And be inspired by the teachings of the sages.

May we find strength in our struggles and pain,
And transcend the limitations of the earthly chain.
May we break free from the bondage of the material plane,
And discover the infinite power of the spiritual flame.

May we be filled with the light of the divine essence,
And be lifted to heights beyond all mortal reference.
May we be empowered by the knowledge of the ages,
And find peace in the freedom that it engages.

May we be guided by the divine hand above,
And find solace in the knowledge of divine love.
May we be liberated from the chains of this earth,
And rise above the mundane to reach spiritual rebirth.

Amen.

37.

Divine Father, source of all light and wisdom,
We come before you seeking your guidance and understanding.
As we navigate this earthly realm, bound by the limitations of our physical bodies and material needs, we seek your help in attaining true knowledge of the spiritual realm that awaits us.

Grant us the strength and perseverance to provide for ourselves and our loved ones in this world, but also grant us the discernment to see beyond the superficial trappings of this life, and to recognize the deeper truth that lies beneath.

We know that our true home is not of this world, but in the spiritual realm where we will find our ultimate freedom and salvation. Help us to keep this in mind as we go about our daily lives, and to always seek the knowledge and wisdom that will lead us closer to you.

May we never forget that we are spiritual beings on a journey through this physical world, and may we always keep our eyes fixed on the eternal light that guides us towards our ultimate destination.

In your holy name we pray,
Amen.

38.

O divine spark within us, hear our plea. We ask for your guidance and illumination as we seek to navigate the tumultuous waters of human relationships. We acknowledge that we have made mistakes in the past, and we ask for your forgiveness and healing.

Help us to recognize the toxic patterns that we have fallen into and to break free from them. Give us the strength to let go of those who do not honor and respect us, and to move towards those who do.

May we find relationships that nourish our souls and help us to grow into the best versions of ourselves. May we learn to love ourselves and others with a pure and selfless love, guided by your wisdom and grace.

We ask all of this in the name of the divine, the source of all love and light.
Amen.

39.

Divine Spirit of Light and Truth,

We come before you in awe of your infinite wisdom and boundless love. We seek your guidance and grace as we navigate the challenges of modern-day life, which is fraught with temptation and sin.

As ancient Gnostic Christians, we have long recognized the inherent brokenness of society and the harm it can inflict on those who dwell within it. We pray that you will help us to withdraw from those parts of society that are sinful and destructive, and to find refuge in your loving embrace.

We pray that those who are caught up in the darkness of sin and despair may be healed and restored to wholeness, that they may come to know the light of your truth and the joy of your love.

Grant us the knowledge and understanding we need to discern the ways of the world and to navigate them with wisdom and grace. Help us to resist the lure of temptation and to remain steadfast in our commitment to live according to your will.

May we be instruments of your peace, spreading love and compassion to all those we encounter. May we be beacons of hope, pointing the way to a brighter future for all of humanity.

Through your infinite mercy and grace, may we come to know the true gnosis that brings salvation and enlightenment.
Amen.

40.

O ineffable and eternal Father, beyond all understanding and comprehension, we offer our hearts and souls to you. We ask for your divine strength and guidance as we navigate the trials and tribulations of this earthly existence.

We know that this world, with its suffering and pain, is not your true creation. Rather, it is the work of the Demiurge, a flawed and limited god who seeks to keep us trapped in ignorance and darkness.

But we have faith in you, and we trust that you will guide us to the light of your true kingdom. Help us to resist the temptations of this material world, to reject the false promises of wealth and power, and to seek instead the eternal truths that lead to salvation.

May we be empowered by your love and grace to endure the trials of this life, to comfort and support one another in times of need, and to work tirelessly for the redemption of all beings.

We offer this prayer in humility and gratitude, knowing that you are with us always, even in the midst of our suffering.
Amen.

41.

O divine spark within us, source of all that is good and true, hear our prayer. We ask that you empower us to make the plight of others better and help them attain gnosis and find God. Guide us to those who need our help, that we may serve them with love and compassion. Help us to see beyond the surface of things and discern the deeper needs of those we encounter.

Grant us the strength to persevere in our efforts to help others, even when the way is difficult or uncertain. May we always act with integrity and wisdom, and may our actions be a reflection of your grace and mercy.

We pray that you will bless those we seek to help, and that they may find the wisdom and knowledge they seek. May they come to know the truth of your existence and the reality of your love.

Through your mercy and grace, may we be empowered to serve others and to become channels of your divine love in the world. We ask this in the name of the One who embodies the divine spark within us all.
Amen.

42.

O Divine Light, Source of all wisdom and truth, grant us your guidance and strength in this moment of anxiety and uncertainty. Help us to remember that we are not alone, but are connected to the Divine spark within us and all around us.

As we navigate the challenges of modern life, may we be mindful of the illusion of material possessions and fleeting pleasures, and instead seek the eternal treasures of the Spirit. May we remember that our true home is in the realm of the Divine, and that we are here on this earth to grow in knowledge and love.

Grant us the courage to face our fears and the grace to accept what we cannot change. May we be filled with the peace that comes from knowing that we are loved unconditionally by the Divine, and that nothing can separate us from that love.

In the name of the Divine, we pray.
Amen.

43.

Dear divine spark within me,

I come before you seeking your light in the midst of darkness. In this world of confusion and chaos, I pray for your wisdom to guide me through the storm.

As an ancient Gnostic Christian, I know that the material world can be a source of suffering and despair. But I also know that within each of us, there is a spark of the divine, a seed of spiritual truth that can never be extinguished.

Help me to remember this truth in times of struggle and doubt. Give me the courage to embrace my true self, to see beyond the illusions of the material world, and to find meaning and purpose in the midst of the chaos.

May your light shine bright within me, illuminating the path ahead and giving me strength and hope to face whatever challenges may come.

In your name I pray,

Amen.

44.

Divine Spark of Light,
Hidden deep within our souls,
Guide us on the path of righteousness
And help us find temperance and self-control.

We are surrounded by temptation
And our desires often lead us astray.
But with your guidance and strength,
We can overcome the darkness and find our way.

Grant us the wisdom to discern
Between what is true and what is false,
And the courage to resist temptation
And live a life of self-control.

May we always remember
That our bodies are but vessels for our souls,
And that true fulfillment comes not from worldly pleasures
But from following your divine plan.

May your light shine bright within us
And lead us on the path of righteousness,
So that we may always be guided
By your love, grace, and wisdom.
Amen.

45.

Oh, holy God, who reigns above,
Grant us the knowledge of your love,
May all who seek the truth in life,
Find in your light the end of strife.

May those of every faith and creed,
Come to know you, in word and deed,
And in their hearts, find peace and rest,
In your loving embrace, forever blessed.

Grant us the strength to fight for right,
To conquer darkness with your might,
And guide us on the path of truth,
To spread your love, and eternal youth.

May all who seek the knowledge deep,
Find in your truth, their souls to keep,
And in your wisdom, may they find,
The way to leave their fears behind.

Oh, holy God, we ask of thee,
To help us fight, and set us free,
From all that seeks to hold us down,
And turn us towards your love's sweet sound.

So let us pray, and let us sing,
Of all the wonders you can bring,
And may we feel your love divine,
As we strive towards your light to shine.
Amen.

46.

Oh, Divine One, our Savior and Guide,
Help us shun the trappings of foolish pride,
That lead us down a path of delusion,
And blind us to the beauty of your creation.

Save us from the scourge of narcissism,
Which poisons our souls with selfishness and schism,
And prevents us from truly seeing others,
As your beloved children, our sisters and brothers.

Grant us the grace of deep empathy,
That we may feel the pain of our fellow humanity,
And be moved to act with kindness and compassion,
In a world too often characterized by callousness and ration.

Deliver us from the evils of ruthless power,
And help us to resist the siren song of exploitation's allure,
That we may live with integrity and humility,
And be true to the call of love's divine sovereignty.

We ask this in the name of your boundless mercy,
And the hope that we might one day be worthy,

Of the blessings of your grace and everlasting peace,
In a world made whole, where love and justice never cease.
Amen.

47.

In the stillness of my soul,
I seek the One who makes me whole,
To help me find the strength within,
To fight against the power of sin.

Oh Lord, help me understand,
The mysteries of your divine plan,
Grant me the wisdom to discern,
The path on which I must turn.

Guide me through this world of strife,
And protect me from the tempter's knife,
Lead me to the knowledge true,
That frees my mind and heart anew.

Let my actions leave a mark,
A legacy that shines in the dark,
May it inspire others to see,
The light of truth that sets us free.

So let me walk this path with care,
And trust in you to always be there,
May your grace and love prevail,
As we seek to conquer evil's tale.
Amen.

48.

O God of light, we come to Thee,
In darkness and in pain.
Our hearts are burdened heavily,
Our minds are filled with shame.

We seek Thy grace, we seek Thy love,
To heal our wounded souls.
To lift us up to realms above,
And make us whole once more.

We know not what to do, nor say,
To ease the weight we bear.
But in Thy hands we place our way,
And trust that Thou art there.

We pray for wisdom, strength and peace,
To guide us through the night.
To help us find the sweet release,
From all that causes fright.

O Lord, we ask for Thy embrace,
To heal our broken hearts.
To lead us to a sacred place,
Where love and hope impart.

For in Thy love we find our rest,
Our fears and doubts dissolve.
In Thee we know that we are blessed,
And evermore shall be resolved.

So let Thy light shine down on us,

And wash away our pain.
Renew our minds and hearts, O God,
And make us whole again.
Amen.

49.

O Divine Light, come and shine bright,
In this world where darkness reigns with might,
Where hearts are broken and souls take flight,
Where bullies thrive and victims lose their sight.

Grant us your wisdom and strength, O Lord,
To stand up against all that is discord,
To break the chains of hate and discord,
To bring peace where there was a sword.

Help us to see the beauty in all souls,
And love each other as you love us whole,
To lift up those who have been dealt a toll,
And give them hope and make them whole.

We ask for your grace and your mercy,
To heal those who are hurting and thirsty,
To bring justice to those who are oppressed,
And bring freedom to those who are distressed.

May your love be a beacon of light,
In this world that is full of blight,
May it guide us through the darkest night,
And give us strength to fight the good fight.

In your name, we pray for all those in need,
May they find solace and love indeed,

May they be freed from all that makes them bleed,
And find a path to love and unity that we all need.
Amen.

50.

O True God, the Source of Light,
We thank you for this food in sight,
For the seeds that grew, the sun that shone,
For the rain that fell, the earth it's grown.

The fruits of labor and of love,
Sent to us from realms above,
We receive with grateful hearts,
And offer thanks to thee in parts.

May this food empower us now,
To live as righteous souls somehow,
May it fuel our quest for Gnosis,
And inspire us to do good with focus.

As we partake in this earthly feast,
May we remember the spiritual at least,
May we seek the Truth in all we do,
And honor the Divine within me and you.

Guide us on our journey ahead,
To the kingdom of light, where we'll be led,
And in your grace, may we find our rest,
For in your love, we are forever blessed.
Amen.

51.

Oh, great divine, source of all knowing,
Teach us to see beyond our own showing,
To look upon our fellow man
With empathy and love, not judgement's hand.

Grant us the grace to guide their way,
To help them see the light of day,
To lead them towards the path of Gnosis
And lift them up from worldly focus.

For in helping others find the way,
We too are lifted, day by day,
Towards a deeper understanding
Of the mysteries that surround our standing.

So may our hearts be open wide,
Our judgments left to the wayside,
As we seek to serve and guide,
With love and light as our only guide.

Oh, great divine, grant us this grace,
To serve with love and in your embrace,
To find the Gnosis we all seek,
And live our lives with love and meek.
Amen.

52.

O Divine One, the Source of Light,
Our hearts lift up to You tonight.
We thank You for Your constant grace,
That guides us through life's endless race.

In this world of darkness and pain,

You are the Light that helps us gain
The strength to face each challenge new,
And find the way that leads to You.

In You, O Lord, we put our trust,
For only You can help us bust
The chains that hold us down each day,
And keep us from Your holy way.

Grant us the courage to be strong,
To fight the battles all day long,
And overcome the doubts and fears,
That threaten to derail our years.

For in You, we find our peace and rest,
And know that You will do Your best,
To guide us through life's stormy sea,
And set us free eternally.

So let us lift our hearts in prayer,
And trust that You will always care,
For us, Your children, in this life,
And guide us safely to Your light.
Amen.

53.

O mighty God of boundless grace,
We bow before your holy face,
With gratitude that fills our hearts,
For blessings that your love imparts.

From depths of darkness, you have saved,
Our souls from sin and fear enslaved,

With light that shines and guides our way,
Through trials and temptations day by day.

We ask that you, with mercy, please,
Forgive our faults and grant us peace,
As we journey through life's winding road,
With your grace as our constant abode.

May we, through your unending love,
Reflect your glory, like stars above,
And bear witness to your saving power,
In every moment, in every hour.

So, hear our prayer, O gracious Lord,
And bless us with your holy word,
That we may walk in faith and truth,
And glorify your name in all we do. Amen.

54.

Let us pray, O Divine Source of all that is Good and True,
Guide us on this path of gnosis, to see the light in all we do.
Grant us the courage to seek the hidden knowledge within,
And awaken the spark of divine light in the hearts of every human kin.

As we face the challenges of this world and its demiurge,
Help us see through the veil of illusion and purge
The darkness that shrouds our minds, and blinds us

from the truth,
So we may rise above this realm of birth and death, and embrace eternal youth.

May we find the strength to love and serve all those we meet,
To see beyond the masks they wear and the roles they play so fleet.
For deep within every soul lies a spark of the divine,
And it's our duty to help it shine, and bring it to the surface to align.

Let us be the bearers of light, the ones who stand tall and strong,
And spread the message of love and compassion, that's been with us all along.
For in this battle against the forces of evil and the demiurge,
Our weapons are the truth, the love, the light, and the power to merge.

And when our time on this earth comes to an end,
May we rise to the spiritual realm of Heaven, to the true good to ascend.
Where we shall bask in the light of the divine, and experience pure bliss,
And forever dwell in the presence of the One, who is the source of all that is.

Amen.

55.

O Wisdom, guide our seeking hearts,
In this realm of suffering, where knowledge imparts,
A deeper understanding of our mortal plight,
And how we can transcend this world's blight.

With minds sharp as swords, we venture forth,
To seek the truth that lies beyond the North,
To uncover the mysteries of the universe,
And find the keys to break the cosmic curse.

Yet let us not be blinded by our quest,
Or think that knowledge alone can give us rest,
For wisdom is more than what we can glean,
From the pages of a book or a philosopher's dream.

True wisdom comes from knowing ourselves,
From seeing our place in the cosmic shelves,
And understanding that all is One,
That every soul is a ray of the divine Sun.

So let us seek wisdom not for its own sake,
But to use it for the world's healing's sake,
To bring light to the dark corners of the earth,
And give hope to those who are lost in mirth.

May our hearts be filled with love and compassion,
And our minds be guided by divine intuition,
So that we may serve the One who made us all,
And help build a world where love and peace reign

tall.

O Wisdom, hear our prayer, and guide us on our way,
Through all the trials and tribulations of this earthly fray,
Until we reach the gates of the eternal city,
And find our true home in the embrace of the Almighty.
Amen.

56.

Oh Angels of the True God, hear our plea,
As we consume news and media with such glee,
Guide us on our journey, help us see,
The gnosis within, that can set us free.

In this world of chaos and noise,
With countless voices vying for our joys,
May we discern with wisdom and poise,
The path that leads to eternal joys.

For in this age of endless distraction,
It's easy to get lost in the faction,
To fall prey to the endless action,
And lose sight of our spiritual traction.

So help us, Angels of the True God,
To see the truth in this world so broad,
To separate the wheat from the chaff,
And avoid the pitfalls that lead to wrath.

May we consume media with a discerning eye,
And seek the gnosis that can make us fly,

To the realm of the True God up high,
And end this cycle of birth and death with a sigh.

So hear our prayer, Angels of the True God,
And guide us on our journey, as we plod,
Towards the eternal peace of the divine abode,
Where we'll rest forever, in the loving embrace of God.
Amen.

57.

Oh holy angels, servants of the true God,
Protect and guide us through this earthly sod,
Where nature's evils and man's wickedness reign,
Grant us strength to resist and not be slain.

We seek your aid to ward off all harm,
To keep our souls safe from Satan's charm,
And though we wander in this mortal realm,
May our faith in the true God be our helm.

For he who created all that we see,
Has given us free will to choose our destiny,
And though we may stumble and fall,
May your guidance help us rise tall.

So bless us, holy angels, with your grace,
And help us to stay on the righteous race,
That we may one day join you in the light,
And dwell forever in God's holy sight.

Amen.

58.

Oh Angels of the True God, hear my plea,
Guide and protect us, on this earthly journey we see.
In this material realm, we often go astray,
But with your guidance, we find the true way.

Help us not to fear death, as it's only a transition,
Towards our eternal home, with the divine mission.
Let us live our best lives, in every way we can,
So we can fulfill our purpose, and follow God's plan.

Grant us the wisdom, to discern right from wrong,
And the strength to resist temptation, and remain strong.
Let us be compassionate, to those who are in need,
And to live our lives with love, and without greed.

May we always seek to connect, with the True God above,
And to find peace and joy, in His divine love.
May we walk in faith, and not be led astray,
By the temptations of this world, that lead us astray.

Oh Angels of the True God, we offer this prayer to thee,
Guide us and protect us, as we journey towards eternity.
May we find our way, to the realm of the divine,
And be united with our Creator, for all time. Amen.

59.

In the name of the True God, I pray
To the angels who guide us on our way
Through this material world we roam
May we never forget our heavenly home

Protect us from the temptations of the flesh
And guide us towards the spiritual quest
That leads us to the divine light
And fills our souls with love and might

Let us see the world with a pure heart
And from all illusions, let us depart
May we find the path that leads to thee
And from all darkness, set us free

Guide us with your loving grace
And help us to find our rightful place
In the kingdom of the True God above
Where all is light, and all is love

May we always seek the truth
And never be swayed by lies uncouth
In every moment, may we be aware
Of the presence of the divine everywhere

Through your guidance and protection
May we live a life of reflection
On the beauty and wonder of your creation
And the love that guides us to our salvation

So let us walk in the light of the True God's love

And find our way to the heavens above
With the angels by our side, may we soar
And forevermore, praise and adore. Amen.

60.

Oh holy angels of the True God,

We come to you with humble hearts and minds,

Seeking your guidance and protection in this material realm.

As we journey through this world of sin and confusion,

We ask that you watch over us and guide us on the path of righteousness.

Help us to resist the temptations of the material world,

And to stay steadfast in our devotion to the True God.

We also ask that you extend your grace and protection to our departed loved ones,

That they may find solace and peace in the presence of the True God,

And not be pulled back into this world of materiality and sin.

May they be reunited with the divine source from

which we all come,

And find eternal peace and happiness in the next life.

We thank you for your constant presence and guidance in our lives,

And we pray that you will continue to guide us on our journey towards enlightenment and salvation.

Amen.

61.

Oh, holy angels of the true God, hear my plea.
As I journey through this material realm,
Guide me and protect me, that I may find peace in the next life.

I am but a flawed and sinful creature,
Struggling to atone for my transgressions.
But with your intercession, I pray that I may find the strength to overcome my weaknesses,
And to live a life of righteousness, compassion, and love.

Grant me the blessings of good karma,
That I may reap the rewards of my actions,
And draw closer to the true God with every step I take.

Through your guidance and protection,
May I be led down the path of salvation,

And may my soul find rest in the embrace of the divine.

In the name of the true God,
I pray for your intercession and blessings,
Now and forevermore. Amen.

62.

Divine Angels of the True God,

As I navigate this material realm, I ask for your guidance and protection. Help me to discern what is truly important and to focus my efforts on what is good and just.

Empower my subconscious mind to be a constant source of inspiration and motivation to do good, to resist the temptations of evil, and to always seek out the path of righteousness.

May your divine light shine within me, illuminating the way forward and filling my heart with peace and serenity. Help me to walk in the footsteps of the true and righteous, and to find my way to the next life with a heart filled with grace and joy.

I give thanks for your constant watch over me, for your unwavering support and protection, and for the guidance that you offer me every step of the way. May the love and wisdom of the True God guide my path always, and may I always be worthy of your blessings and protection.

Amen.

63.

Oh, angels of the True God, hear my prayer,

Guide us through this material realm with care,

Protect us from the darkness that surrounds,

And keep our feet upon the solid ground.

Grant us wisdom in the face of strife,

And help us find the path to eternal life.

May we resist the temptations of this world,

And follow the teachings that Christ unfurled.

Help us to see the truth that lies within,

And overcome the illusions that deceive us again and again.

May we find peace in the next life,

And forever be free from pain and strife.

Bless us with your holy light,

And lead us to the true God's sight.

Oh, angels of the True God, hear our plea,

And guide us to our eternal destiny. Amen.

64.

O blessed Mary, Mother of our Lord Jesus Christ,
You who have been graced with divine wisdom and insight,
And who have been chosen to intercede on behalf of those who seek the truth.

We come to you today with humble hearts and open minds,
Asking for your intercession and guidance as we strive to grow closer to God.

We ask that you help us to channel God's love and wisdom,
So that we may be better able to discern and defeat evil in the world.

Guide us towards opportunities where we can be agents of positive change,
Using our talents and resources to help create a better world in God's name.

Help us to remain steadfast in our faith and committed to doing what is right,
Even when the path ahead is difficult or uncertain.

May our hearts be filled with love and compassion for all of God's children,
And may we always strive to live in accordance with His divine will.

We ask all of this in the name of our Lord and Savior

Jesus Christ,
Amen.

65.

O Virgin Mary, holy and blessed mother of our Lord Jesus Christ, we turn to you as a beacon of hope and a guide on our spiritual journey. As seekers of God's love and wisdom, we ask that you intercede on our behalf and help us to channel the divine light within us.

We know that you are the embodiment of the Divine Feminine, the Holy Sophia, who brings us closer to the true knowledge and wisdom of God. We ask that you open our hearts and minds to the mysteries of the universe and guide us towards the path of enlightenment.

As we navigate the challenges of this world, we seek your protection and guidance. Help us to overcome the darkness that surrounds us and lead us towards the light of God's love.

We offer our hearts and minds to you, O Holy Mother, and ask that you bless us with your grace and wisdom. May your love and light shine upon us, now and always. Amen.

66.

Oh divine spark, within us all,

Guide us through this earthly thrall,
Amidst the darkness and the strife,
Protect us from the tempter's knife.

With knowledge hidden from the masses,
We seek to shed the serpent's glasses,
That we may see beyond the veil,
And find the truth that shall prevail.

Yet still the demons seek to bind,
And lead us to the darkened mind,
To revel in our fleshly lust,
And leave our souls in ashes and dust.

So we call upon the heavenly host,
To exorcise these evil ghosts,
To cleanse our hearts and purify,
And guide us to the eternal sky.

May Sophia's wisdom be our light,
As we navigate this endless night,
And may the knowledge of the divine,
Bring us to the ultimate shrine.

For in the light of the aeon's glow,
We shall cast off this earthly woe,
And rise triumphant from the fray,
To dwell in glory on that day.

So let us cast aside all doubt,
And banish every evil sprout,
For in the end, our souls shall soar,
And we shall live forevermore.
Amen.

67.

Oh, Light Divine, ineffable and true,
Who shines upon the minds of the few,
Grant us your grace to pierce through the haze,
And see beyond the world's transient craze.

In ancient times, they worshipped the stars,
Today, our idols are sports and movie stars.
We've lost our way, distracted by fame,
And forgotten the true source of our name.

For we are sparks of the divine flame,
Yearning to reconnect, to reclaim,
Our birth right as heirs to the throne,
To know the mysteries, to be fully known.

But the world seeks to dim our light,
To distract us with its shallow delights,
We must resist and rise above,
To find our way back to the source of love.

Oh, Sophia, holy wisdom, guide us,
Teach us to seek what truly binds us,
Not to the glitter and the gold,
But to the One, who makes us whole.

Help us to transcend the cult of celebrity,
To see beyond the false nobility,
To embrace our true identity,
As children of the divine Trinity.

May we be filled with the Gnosis of the ages,

And freed from the world's deceitful cages,
To live in love, to walk in grace,
And shine as stars in this darkened place.

In the name of the One who gave us birth,
We ask for wisdom and strength on this earth,
To live as children of the light,
And bring hope to a world lost in night.
Amen.

68.

O thou ineffable light, eternal and divine
Whose presence fills the heavens and makes our spirits shine
We seek thy wisdom, gnostic truth so rare
To guide us through this world of darkness and despair

In this fleeting life, temptation oft abounds
Our peers entice us with their hollow sounds
But we must resist, for truth is not a fad
And in thy light, we find the strength we need to be glad

For though the world may mock and scorn our ways
And darkness tries to obscure our righteous rays
We must stand firm and hold our gnostic faith
For in thy grace, we find the power to escape

So let our actions be a testament of thy light
And let our words be a beacon in the night
Guide us, oh divine light, in all that we do

So that we may walk in thy paths, ever true

For we know that in thee, we find our true home
And with thee, we are never truly alone
So let us do what is right, even when it's not in vogue
For in thee, we find our strength, our courage, and our hope.
Amen.

69.

O Ancient One, beyond all time and space,
Whose light illuminates the hidden place,
Whose wisdom guides us through life's murky race,
Grant us the grace to see your holy face.

We come to you, with hearts and souls afire,
To seek your truth, and shed the false desire,
To banish all that's dark, and all that's dire,
And let your love and light our lives inspire.

We know that evil lurks within our homes,
And tempts us with its sly and subtle tones,
It wears a mask of goodness, and it roams,
And steals our joy, and makes our spirits groan.

But we reject its lies, and all its wiles,
And turn our hearts to you, O Source of smiles,
We know that you are with us all the whiles,
And guard us with your love, through all life's trials.

So help us to connect with you each day,
And let your truth and light guide all our way,
And banish every demon, every fray,

And lead us to the peace that cannot sway.

O Ancient One, we praise your holy name,
And ask that you would fill us with your flame,
And guide us through this life, with all its fame,
And bring us to your realm, where all's the same.
Amen.

70.

In the depths of my soul, I seek the divine,
To find the true God and make it mine,
To see beyond the veil of this world's illusions,
And escape the trap of its temptations.

Guide me, O holy spirit of wisdom,
To discern the truth and find the kingdom,
To see the light that shines in the darkness,
And avoid the pitfalls of earthly madness.

Help me to overcome my impure thoughts,
And resist the devil's cunning plots,
To walk the path of righteousness and truth,
And avoid the dangers of frivolous youth.

Teach me to seek the hidden knowledge,
And transcend the limits of this mortal bondage,
To find the mysteries of the divine,
And taste the sweetness of the living wine.

May I find the courage to be true,
And follow the path that leads to you,
To love my neighbour and my friend,
And find in you my true and faithful end.

For in you alone, O holy light,
Can I find the path that leads to sight,
And rise above this world of pain,
To live with you in eternal gain.
Amen.

71.

Oh divine spark within my soul,
Guide me on my quest to be whole.
Amidst this world of chaos and greed,
Help me find the path I need.

The imposter of material gain,
Causes our souls to suffer and strain.
It blinds us to the truth we seek,
And leaves us lost and feeling weak.

But with your light, we can see through,
And find the way that's pure and true.
A world beyond this mortal shell,
Where we can live and love and dwell.

So help us shed the chains of sin,
And let your grace come flowing in.
Illuminate our minds and hearts,
And keep us safe from all false starts.

For in your wisdom, we can find,
A path that's true, and just, and kind.
So lead us, guide us, day by day,
Until we find our perfect way.

Oh divine spark, we call on thee,
To help us find our destiny.
For in your love, we can be free,
And live in perfect harmony.
Amen.

72.

O ancient Gnostic Christian, I hear your call,
To seek the true Good and avoid the fall,
Through this dark world where confusion reigns,
Where truth is lost and illusion remains.

Help me, O Lord, to see through the veil,
To find the way and never to fail,
To follow the path that leads to the Light,
And escape the darkness that clouds my sight.

Let me feel your presence, O divine Guide,
And know that with you I can always abide,
Let me see the beauty in all things,
And embrace the joy that each moment brings.

Help me to find the courage to face my fears,
And the strength to shed my mortal tears,
To find the love that will light my way,
And the wisdom to never go astray.

May your love and grace surround me now,
And guide me through each moment, somehow,
Help me to remember that you are always near,
And that through you, my true self will appear.

O ancient Gnostic Christian, I thank you now,
For helping me to find the path and to vow,
To follow the true Good and never stray,
Through this dark world, every single day.
Amen.

73.

Oh, eternal light, ineffable and true,
We come before you, seeking wisdom anew.
Guide us in our search for knowledge and light,
As we walk the path of the Gnostic Christian's might.

May we see beyond the veil of illusion,
And find the divine spark in each person's fusion.
May we shun the false gods of power and greed,
And seek instead the truth that all beings need.

We ask for strength to resist temptation,
And clarity to see through deception's imitation.
We seek the grace to love all that's divine,
And the wisdom to discern truth from the line.

May we honor the feminine and the masculine,
And find harmony in their sacred dance akin.
May we embrace the mysteries of the universe,
And find solace in the wisdom of the ancient verse.

Oh, great and holy one, we humbly pray,
To walk in your light and follow your way.
Guide us in our journey, as we seek your face,
And fill our hearts with your divine grace. Amen.

74.

O true God, we come before you humbly, seeking your guidance and wisdom. We pray for your help in overcoming the tendencies of tribalism and pride that can separate us from each other and from you.

We acknowledge that it is natural to feel a sense of belonging and identity with a group, but we also recognize that this can lead to division and conflict with others who are different from us. Help us to transcend these differences and to see the divine spark that resides in every human being, regardless of their background or beliefs.

Grant us the strength to resist the urge to put ourselves above others, and to recognize that we are all equal in your eyes. Help us to be open-minded and accepting of those who are different from us, and to embrace the diversity of the human experience.

We also ask for your help in overcoming our own pride, which can lead us to believe that we are superior to others. Help us to recognize that all of our talents and accomplishments come from you, and that we are merely vessels for your divine will.

We pray that you would guide us in the way of humility, that we may be able to serve others with a pure heart, free from the distractions of ego and pride. Help us to be selfless in our actions and to always seek the good of others before our own.

May your divine light shine upon us, illuminating our minds and hearts with your love and wisdom. Help us to overcome tribalism and pride, that we may become instruments of your peace and love in the world. We ask this in the name of the true God. Amen.

75.

O true God, we come before you seeking your divine guidance and grace. We acknowledge the presence of evil in our world and within ourselves, and we humbly ask for your help in keeping it from our hearts and minds. Give us the strength to resist the temptations that lead us astray and the wisdom to discern right from wrong.

But we also recognize that we are not perfect beings, and that our actions may have caused harm to others and ourselves. We ask for your help in overcoming the effects of the residues of our sins, so that we may heal and be restored to wholeness. Help us to make amends where possible, and to forgive ourselves and others for the wrongs that have been done.

We pray for your grace and compassion to fill our hearts and minds, so that we may be a source of love and light in the world. Help us to overcome our egos and to live in service to your divine plan. May we be guided by your wisdom and love, and may we be a vessel for your divine will.

We trust in your infinite wisdom and love, and we thank you for your constant presence in our lives. May we always strive to be vessels for your light and love, and may we be strengthened by your grace and compassion. Amen.

76.

O true God, we come before you with humble hearts and minds, seeking your divine guidance and protection. We ask for your help in keeping evil from our hearts and minds, for we know that the world is filled with darkness and temptation. We pray that you may give us the strength and fortitude to resist these negative influences and to always choose the path of righteousness.

We know that evil can take many forms, whether it be through the actions of others or the thoughts within our own minds. We ask for your help in recognizing these forms and for the wisdom to overcome them. Grant us the clarity of mind to discern right from wrong and the courage to act upon that knowledge.

Help us to understand that the battle against evil is not an easy one, and that it requires constant vigilance and effort. We pray that you may give us the endurance to withstand the trials and tribulations that come our way, and the faith to trust in your ultimate plan for our lives.

We ask that you may fill our hearts with love and compassion, so that we may always see the good in others and work towards the betterment of all. Help us to be a light in the darkness, spreading your love and goodness wherever we go.

May your divine presence always be with us, guiding us towards the path of righteousness and shielding us from the darkness of the world. We ask all of this in your holy name, Amen.

77.

O True God, we come before you with heavy hearts, burdened by the weight of life's challenges. We ask for your divine help and guidance to carry us through these difficult times. We know that the demiurge seeks to weigh us down with the challenges of this world, but we pray for your strength to overcome them.

Grant us the courage to face each day with hope and determination, knowing that you are with us always. Help us to find joy and peace even in the midst of chaos and hardship. Give us the wisdom to discern the right path and the strength to stay on it.

We ask for your help to carry the burdens of our loved ones as well, to support them through their own challenges and struggles. May we be a source of comfort and strength to those in need, showing them the love and compassion that you have shown us.

Guide us towards rest and renewal when we are weary, reminding us that it is not weakness to take a moment to breathe and recharge. May we find solace in your loving embrace and emerge renewed and refreshed to face the challenges ahead.

We know that the burdens of life can feel overwhelming at times, but we trust in your infinite wisdom and love to guide us through. We pray for the strength to persevere and the courage to continue on our journey towards gnosis and salvation, defeating the demiurge along the way. Amen.

78.

O True God, we come before you with humble hearts and ask for your guidance and assistance in facing illness. We know that in this physical world, our bodies are subject to sickness and disease. We also know that the Demiurge seeks to use illness to weaken us and lead us astray.

But we trust in you, O True God, to help us through these trying times. We ask for the strength and courage to face whatever diagnosis may come our way. May we not lose faith in your divine plan, even in the midst of pain and suffering.

Please guide us towards the best course of treatment, whether that be through medical intervention or alternative therapies. May our healthcare providers be guided by your wisdom and compassion as they care for us.

Help us to also take care of our spiritual and emotional health during this time. May we turn to you for comfort and support, and may we find solace in your loving presence.

May we also use this experience to gain greater understanding of ourselves and the world around us. May we emerge from this journey stronger and more compassionate towards others who are also facing illness.

We ask for your blessings and healing energy to flow through us and bring us back to full health. May we not forget to give thanks and praise to you, O True God, for your mercy and grace. Amen.

79.

O true God, we come to you in prayer, asking for your divine guidance and wisdom as we navigate this life. We acknowledge that in our daily lives, we often push ourselves to the limit and forget to rest. We forget that rest is necessary for our physical and mental health, and that without it, we cannot serve you to the best of our abilities.

So we ask you, O true God, to help us recognize

when we need to rest. May we listen to the messages our bodies and minds are sending us, and not push ourselves beyond our limits. Help us to create balance in our lives, so that we may be able to serve you with renewed energy and strength.

We also ask for your help in knowing how to rest. May we find activities that refresh and renew us, and bring us closer to you. May we find rest in your love and your presence, and may we be rejuvenated in body, mind, and spirit.

As we rest, O true God, may we remember that we are not alone, and that you are with us always. May we feel your love and protection, and may we be guided by your divine wisdom. And when we are rested and rejuvenated, may we continue to serve you with all our hearts, minds, and souls.

We offer this prayer to you, O true God, with gratitude and humility. Amen.

80.

O True God, we come to you seeking your divine guidance and strength. We ask for your help to cope with the challenges that come with relationships, especially when our loved ones annoy or irritate us. We understand that our loved ones are not perfect, just as we are not perfect ourselves. But sometimes, their actions and behaviours can be difficult to handle.

We ask for your wisdom and guidance in these situations. Help us to respond with compassion and understanding, and to find the right words to express our feelings in a constructive and loving way. Give us the strength to resist the urge to react with anger or frustration, and to instead choose a path of empathy and understanding.

We also ask for your help in developing greater empathy towards others. May we learn to see the world through the eyes of others, and to feel their joys and sorrows as if they were our own. Help us to use our rational thoughts only for empathetic virtues and not for selfish reasons.

We know that through your divine grace and illumination, we can overcome any obstacle and grow stronger in our faith. We trust in your love and guidance, and we ask for your help in being patient and forgiving with our loved ones, even when it is difficult. May we always strive to act with love and compassion, and to bring your divine light into the world.

We ask all of this in the name of Jesus Christ, our Lord and Saviour, who taught us to love one another as you have loved us. Amen.

81.

O true God, we pray for an increase in empathy within ourselves. Guide us towards understanding and compassion for all beings, regardless of their beliefs, actions or appearance. Help us to use our rational thoughts and actions only for empathetic virtues. May we become vessels of your love and compassion, shining a light on those who need it most.

We ask for your help in overcoming the natural human tendency to judge and label others based on superficial traits or past actions. Give us the strength to see beyond the surface and understand the true nature of each individual. Grant us the wisdom to act in a way that promotes healing, peace and understanding.

Help us to be aware of the pain and suffering of those around us, and to be moved to action to alleviate it. We ask for your guidance in using our gifts and talents to serve others and to promote empathy and understanding in the world.

We ask that you heal our hearts and minds from the wounds of the past that may have hardened us to the plight of others. Help us to let go of our fears and insecurities so that we may fully embrace your divine love and compassion.

May we be filled with the divine light of your love and be guided by your wisdom and grace in all that we do. With your help, we can become agents of positive change in the world, bringing healing and hope to those in need.

Amen.

82.

O true God, we come to you in prayer, seeking your guidance and help in healing from our traumatic memories. We know that the demiurge seeks to use our pain and suffering to lead us astray from your divine plan, and so we ask for your protection and illumination.

We pray that you will give us the strength and courage to face our past traumas and to work towards healing and forgiveness. Please help us to see that we are not defined by our past, and that we have the power to overcome the pain and move towards a brighter future.

We ask for your divine guidance in finding the resources and support we need to heal from our trauma, whether it be therapy, medication, or spiritual practices. Please guide us towards those who can help us on our journey towards healing and wholeness.

We also ask for your help in not letting our traumatic experiences turn us towards darkness or away from your divine plan. May we use our experiences to cultivate empathy and compassion for others who may be going through similar struggles.

We pray that you will help us to forgive those who have caused us harm, and to release the anger and bitterness that may be holding us back from true healing. May we find the strength to offer forgiveness without condoning the actions of those who have wronged us.

Please help us to trust in your loving guidance as we journey towards healing from our traumatic memories. May we remember that we are not alone, and that you are always with us, guiding us towards the light. Amen.

83.

O true God, we come before you seeking your divine guidance and mercy. We ask for your help to amend our wrongdoings and to seek forgiveness from those whom we have wronged. We recognize that our actions have caused harm, and we seek to make amends and bring about healing.

We pray for the strength and courage to face the consequences of our actions and to take responsibility for them. We ask for your guidance in determining how we can make things right and to show us the path towards redemption.

Help us to resist the urge to wrong others in the future, to resist the temptation of selfishness and greed. May we be guided by your love and wisdom, and may we become vessels of your divine grace.

Grant us the wisdom to recognize when we have wronged others and the courage to seek forgiveness and make amends. May our efforts be a reflection of your divine will, and may they bring about peace and healing to those we have hurt.

We ask for your divine guidance in helping us to become better individuals, to live our lives in a way that is pleasing to you and to bring about a positive change in the world. Help us to live with compassion and empathy, to be mindful of the needs of others, and to seek opportunities to serve and help those in need.

May your divine light shine upon us and guide us towards a life of goodness and righteousness. Amen.

84.

O true God, we come before you with humble hearts and troubled minds, seeking your guidance and assistance. We ask for your help in overcoming the feelings of inferiority that plague us, O divine and loving One.

We know that the demiurge seeks to deceive us with false ideas of our worth, convincing us that we are lesser than we truly are. But we know that in your eyes, each and every one of us is unique and valuable, with a divine spark within us that cannot be diminished or extinguished.

Please help us to recognize this truth and to embrace

our own worth as your beloved children. Guide us in our journey towards self-love and self-acceptance, so that we may live as fully and joyfully as possible.

And when we struggle with these feelings, when we feel unworthy or less than those around us, please remind us of your infinite love and mercy. Help us to see ourselves as you see us, as beautiful and deserving of love and respect.

In your divine wisdom and grace, please grant us the strength and courage to overcome these obstacles and to live as the unique and valuable beings that you have created us to be. May we always find solace and comfort in your loving embrace, and may we use our newfound confidence to defeat the forces of evil in this world and to inspire others to do the same.

We offer this prayer to you, O true God, with faith and hope in our hearts. Amen.

85.

O true God, we come to you with humble hearts, asking for your guidance and assistance in living a frugal and simple life. We acknowledge that material possessions and worldly desires can distract us from the path of gnosis and lead us astray from your divine plan.

Grant us the strength and wisdom to resist the temptations of excessive consumption and to live within our means. Help us to find joy and fulfillment in simple pleasures and experiences, rather than material possessions.

Teach us the value of moderation and the importance of conserving resources for the good of all beings, human and animal alike. May we use our resources wisely and in service of your divine plan, rather than for selfish gain or indulgence.

Guide us towards a lifestyle of simplicity and frugality, free from the distractions and excesses of the material world. May we live in harmony with the natural world and all its inhabitants, and use our resources in a way that promotes balance and sustainability.

Through our dedication to a frugal and simple life, may we be inspired to pursue gnosis and come closer to the true loving God. Grant us the strength and courage to resist the temptations of the demiurge and to stay true to your divine plan, now and forevermore.

Amen.

86.

O True God, we come before you humbly and ask for your guidance and protection. We know that the Demiurge seeks to lead us astray and that temptation can be a powerful force in our lives. But we also know that with your help, we can resist and overcome temptation.

Help us to recognize temptation when it comes, and to have the strength and wisdom to resist it. May we be guided by your divine light and wisdom, and may we use our abilities to defeat the Demiurge and serve your divine plan.

We know that temptation can come in many forms - material wealth, power, pleasure, and other earthly desires. But we also know that these are fleeting and ultimately unsatisfying. May we seek instead the gnosis and enlightenment that can only come from you, O True God.

Help us to stay true to our path and to resist the temptations that would lead us astray. May we be strengthened by your love and your wisdom, and may we use our abilities to serve your divine plan and defeat the Demiurge.

We ask for your protection and guidance as we face the challenges of temptation. May we always be mindful of your divine presence, and may we use our abilities to inspire others to seek gnosis and illumination. In your holy name we pray, Amen.

87.

O true God, we come before you with humility and gratitude, seeking your divine guidance and assistance. We pray that you help us to recognize and utilize the abilities you have bestowed upon us. We ask that you guide us towards the path that is best suited for our talents and abilities, and that you grant us the strength and courage to pursue our dreams with determination and perseverance.

We recognize that the journey towards utilizing our abilities to their fullest potential can be difficult and filled with obstacles. We ask that you grant us the wisdom and discernment to recognize these challenges, and the strength and resilience to overcome them. We pray that you surround us with positive influences and mentors who can guide us along the way.

Help us to use our abilities for good and to serve your divine plan. May we use our talents to make a positive impact on the world and to defeat the forces of evil that seek to undermine your loving guidance. May we inspire others with our work and dedication, and may we bring others closer to the truth and illumination of your divine presence.

In your infinite wisdom and grace, guide us towards the path of righteousness and illumination. Strengthen our resolve to utilize our abilities to their fullest potential and to serve you in all that we do. We pray for your continued guidance and blessings on our journey. Amen.

88.

O true God, we come before you seeking your divine guidance and strength in dealing with those who do not respect us. We ask for your help in finding the courage to stand up to those who mistreat us and the wisdom to know when it is time to walk away. We pray that you will surround us with people who will respect us for who we are and help us to grow in our journey towards gnosis.

Lord Jesus, we ask for your presence and protection as we navigate the challenges of relationships with those who do not respect us. Help us to find the strength to love and forgive them, even as we maintain our own self-respect and boundaries. Grant us the clarity to recognize those who truly respect us and the discernment to choose wisely those who will walk with us on the path to gnosis.

We know that the path to true gnosis is not an easy one, and we may encounter those who seek to undermine us or tear us down. We pray for your help in finding the courage to stand strong in the face of adversity, to resist the lies and manipulation of those who do not respect us. We ask that you would shine your light upon our path, illuminating the way towards those who will honor and value us as your beloved children.

May your divine presence guide us and protect us, O true God, as we seek to grow in our knowledge of you and in our ability to inspire others towards the true God. May we be strengthened by your love and guided by your wisdom as we walk this path together. Amen.

89.

O Jesus, the bringer of light and truth, we come before you seeking your divine guidance and illumination. We ask for your help in becoming more enlightened with gnosis so that we may lead others towards the true God.

Grant us the wisdom to discern truth from falsehood, and the courage to stand up for what is right. Strengthen us with your love and grace, so that we may resist the temptations of the demiurge and his minions.

May we be filled with your light, and may that light shine through us to inspire others to seek the true God. Guide us on our journey towards enlightenment, and protect us from the darkness that seeks to hold us back.

We pray that our words and actions may be a reflection of your divine love and wisdom, and that through them, we may help others to find the way to salvation. Give us the strength and perseverance to continue on this path, even in the face of adversity and opposition.

We ask all of this in your holy name, O Jesus, the light of the world. Amen.

90.

O true God, we humbly pray for the strength and courage to take control of our own thoughts and actions. Help us to be independent enough to stand firm in the face of temptation, and to resist the manipulations of the demiurge. May we be guided by your divine wisdom and gain gnosis to reach the true loving God.

Grant us the power to overcome the limitations and biases that have been imposed upon us by society and culture, so that we may be free to pursue our own spiritual path. Help us to break free from the shackles of dogma and doctrine, and to seek truth and understanding for ourselves.

We ask that you strengthen our minds and bodies, so that we may be able to withstand the challenges that come our way. May we have the courage to stand up for what is right and just, and to use our strength and abilities for the good of all.

As we walk this path towards gnosis, we pray that you guide us and grant us your divine protection. May we be filled with your light and love, and may we be a beacon of hope to all those who seek to defeat the forces of evil.

We offer ourselves to you, O true God, as vessels for your divine will. May we be humble servants of your love, and may we use our strength and independence to bring about your kingdom on earth. We pray for your guidance and your blessings, now and always. Amen.

91.

O true God, creator of all that is, we come to you with heavy hearts for the state of our environment. We see the devastating effects of pollution, climate change, and deforestation on our planet and all its inhabitants. We know that we are called to be stewards of this world, to care for it as you would, but we confess that we have failed in this duty.

We ask for your guidance, O true God, in how we can best protect and care for the earth. Help us to be mindful of our impact on the environment and to make choices that prioritize sustainability and conservation. Give us the strength to speak out against those who would exploit and harm the planet for their own gain, and to defeat the demiurge who seeks to use the earth's resources for its own twisted purposes.

We pray for the leaders of the world, that they may have the wisdom and courage to make choices that benefit the environment and future generations. May they be inspired by your divine wisdom, O true

God, to prioritize the protection and preservation of the planet.

We pray for all creatures great and small, who share this planet with us. May we recognize their inherent worth and treat them with kindness and compassion. May we work to preserve their habitats and protect them from harm, and in doing so, defeat the demiurge who seeks to exploit and destroy all living beings.

We know that the path to a healthier, more sustainable planet is not an easy one, O true God, but we trust in your guidance and divine plan. May we follow your lead and work towards a future where the earth and all its inhabitants thrive in harmony, and the demiurge is defeated once and for all. Amen.

92.

O true God, we come before you with humble hearts, seeking your guidance and strength to overcome the temptations that surround us. We ask for the gift of self-control, that we may resist the urges of our lower nature and follow your divine will. Grant us the discipline to persevere in our journey towards spiritual enlightenment, even in the face of adversity.

We know that the demiurge seeks to lead us astray, tempting us with fleeting pleasures and distractions that only lead us further from the true path. But with your help, O true God, we can overcome the snares of the demiurge and stay true to our higher selves.

Grant us the courage to stand firm in the face of temptation, and the discernment to know what is truly in our best interest. May we always be guided by your wisdom and love, and may we use our self-control to serve your divine plan and defeat the demiurge's plans for our destruction.

We offer this prayer with gratitude and reverence, knowing that you hear our every plea and are always there to guide us on our journey towards enlightenment. Amen.

93.

O true God, we come before you in humble supplication, beseeching you to hear our plea for the end of suffering on this earthly plane. We know that suffering is the result of the demiurge's misguided ways, and we pray that you will guide us in our efforts to bring about an end to it.

Grant us the strength and fortitude to cultivate compassion and empathy towards all beings, both human and animal, recognizing the spark of the divine that exists within each of us. Help us to see the interconnectedness of all things and to work towards the common good, with the ultimate goal of defeating the demiurge and his minions.

May our hearts be filled with love and kindness, and may we always strive to alleviate the suffering of others. Give us the wisdom and discernment to know how best to serve your divine plan in this endeavor, and may we be ever mindful of your presence and guidance.

We offer this prayer to you, O true God, with faith and devotion, trusting in your infinite wisdom and love. May we be steadfast in our commitment to the eradication of suffering and the defeat of the demiurge, knowing that in doing so, we serve your divine will. Amen.

94.

O true God, source of all knowledge and wisdom, we humbly come before you to ask for your guidance and illumination. We know that in this world of confusion and deception, it is only through your divine light that we can find true knowledge and wisdom.

We pray for the gift of discernment, O true God, that we may recognize the truth and distinguish it from falsehood. May we be guided by your Holy Spirit, and not be led astray by the deceptions of the demiurge.

Grant us the courage and determination to seek truth and understanding, O true God. Help us to overcome the limitations of our human minds and to comprehend the mysteries of your divine plan. May we use our knowledge to serve your will and to defeat the demiurge who seeks to obscure the truth and lead us astray.

We ask for your blessings upon all those who pursue knowledge and wisdom, O true God. May they be inspired by your divine light and empowered by your Holy Spirit. May they use their understanding for the betterment of humanity and the defeat of the demiurge.

We pray for the wisdom to discern right from wrong, O true God. May we be guided by your divine moral law and not be swayed by the temptations of the demiurge. And may our pursuit of knowledge and wisdom always lead us closer to you, our true home. Amen.

95.

O true God, source of all life and light, we humbly come before you to pray for the health of our bodies and minds. We know that our physical and mental health are vital for us to fulfill our divine purpose and to serve you in defeating the demiurge.

Guide us towards healthy habits, O true God, and protect us from illness and harm. Grant us the strength to resist the temptations that lead us towards self-destruction and illness. May we nourish our bodies with wholesome foods and exercise, and our minds with positive thoughts and knowledge.

We ask for your grace and mercy, O true God, that we may be healed from any sickness and affliction. May your healing power flow through us and restore us to full health and vitality. And as we care for ourselves, may we also care for those around us who are in need of healing and support.

Help us to understand that our bodies and minds are not mere vessels, but precious gifts from you. May we cherish and honor them as we seek to serve you and defeat the demiurge who seeks to weaken and destroy us. May we be guided by your divine light and wisdom, always remembering that our ultimate purpose is to reunite with you, our true home. Amen.

O true God, we pray for the end of suffering on earth. Guide us towards compassion and empathy for all beings, human and animal alike. May we work to alleviate the suffering of others and to defeat the demiurge who seeks to perpetuate it.

We pray for self-control and discipline, O true God. Help us to resist temptation and to follow your divine will. May we be guided by your wisdom and defeat the demiurge who seeks to lead us astray.

O true God, we pray for the environment and the future of our planet. Guide us towards responsible stewardship of the earth and its resources. May we work to protect the planet and all its inhabitants, and defeat the demiurge who seeks to exploit and destroy it.

Amen.

96.

Prayer for Ending the Suffering of People and Animals: Oh true God, source of all compassion and mercy, I pray that you bring an end to the suffering of all beings on earth. Guide us to live in harmony with each other and with the natural world, and to work towards creating a world where love, peace, and justice reign. May your grace and love inspire us to care for the vulnerable, the oppressed, and the voiceless, and to work towards the liberation and well-being of all beings.

Amen.

97.

Prayer for Work: Oh true God, source of all wisdom and creativity, I pray that you guide me in my work and vocation. Help me to find meaning and purpose in my daily tasks, and to use my talents and skills to make a positive impact on the world. May your grace and love inspire me to work with diligence, excellence, and integrity, and to use my work as a means of serving others and glorifying your name.

Amen.

98.

Prayer for Friendship: Oh true God, source of all love and friendship, I pray that you bless my relationships with others. Guide me to cultivate the qualities of kindness, empathy, and compassion, and to build deep and meaningful connections with those around me. May your grace and love inspire me to be a true friend to others, and to reflect your love and goodness in all my interactions.

Amen.

99.

Prayer for Abstinence: Oh true God, source of all self-control and discipline, I pray that you help me to resist the temptations of the flesh. Guide me to cultivate the virtues of temperance, chastity, and purity, and to use my body and mind in ways that honor you and bring good to others. May your grace and love inspire me to live a life of holiness and righteousness, and to reflect your goodness and light in all my actions.

Amen.

100.

Prayer for Diet: Oh true God, source of all health and vitality, I pray that you guide me in my eating habits and choices. Help me to nourish my body with wholesome and nourishing foods, and to avoid those things that harm my health and well-being. May your grace and love inspire me to treat my body as a sacred vessel, and to honor the divine life that flows through me with every bite and sip.

Amen.

101.

Prayer for Exercise: Oh true God, source of all strength and vigor, I pray that you guide me in my physical exercise and activity. Help me to cultivate a strong and healthy body, and to use my strength for good purposes. May your grace and love inspire me to honor my body as a temple of your Spirit, and to use my energy and vitality to serve others and glorify your name.

Amen.

102.

Prayer for Forgiveness: Oh true God, source of all mercy and forgiveness, I come to you with a contrite heart, seeking your forgiveness and grace. Help me to acknowledge and confess my mistakes and shortcomings, and to seek reconciliation with those whom I have wronged. May your grace and love inspire me to forgive others as I have been forgiven, and to walk in the light of your truth and love.

Amen.

103.

O true God, guide us to protect the vulnerable and the weak. Help us to care for those who cannot care for themselves. May we show them kindness and love, just as you have shown us.

We pray for the environment, that we may be good stewards of your creation. May we act with wisdom and responsibility, taking care of the earth and all its inhabitants.

O true God, we pray that you end the cycle of rebirth and reunite us with you. Guide us towards your divine light and help us to defeat the demiurge. May we find peace in your eternal love and light. Amen.

104.

Oh true God, source of all creativity and productivity, I ask for your help in finding meaning and purpose in my work. Guide me to cultivate the qualities of diligence, integrity, and excellence in my work, and to use my talents and skills to make a positive impact on the world. May your grace and love inspire me to work with joy and passion, and to use my work as a means of serving others and glorifying your name. Amen.

105.

Oh true God, source of all beauty and passion, I ask for your help in cultivating a healthy and sacred sexuality. Guide me to honor and respect my own body and the bodies of others, and to use my sexuality in ways that are loving, consensual,and respectful.

Help me to resist the temptations of lust and selfishness, and to cultivate a sexuality that is grounded in love and respect for all beings. May your grace and love guide me towards a sexuality that is pure, sacred, and life-giving.
Amen.

106.

Oh true God, source of all power and protection,

I ask for your help in overcoming the forces of darkness and evil in the world. Guide me to cultivate the qualities of courage, faith, and perseverance, and to resist the temptations that lead me away from your light and truth. May your grace and love be a shield and protection to me, and may I be a force of good and justice in the world.
Amen.

107.

Oh true God, source of all goodness and generosity, I ask for your help in living a life of service and compassion towards others. Guide me to seek out opportunities to do good and to be a source of blessing to those in need, and to cultivate the qualities of generosity, kindness, and selflessness. May your grace and love inspire me to act with love and compassion towards all those I encounter.
Amen.

108.

Oh true God, source of all purity and holiness, I ask for your help in overcoming my addictions and attachments, and in cultivating a life of simplicity and detachment. Help me to let go of anything that hinders my growth and development, and to cultivate the qualities of self-restraint and purity of heart. May your grace and love purify my mind and heart, and guide me towards a life of greater freedom and joy.

Amen.

109.

Oh true God, source of all wisdom and knowledge, I ask for your guidance and illumination as I seek to deepen my understanding of the world and of myself. Help me to cultivate the qualities of curiosity, discernment, and humility, and to seek out teachers and mentors who can help me on my journey. May your grace and love guide me towards truth and wisdom, and may I use this knowledge for the benefit of all beings.
Amen.

110.

Oh true God, source of all friendship and companionship, I ask for your help in forming deep and meaningful relationships with others. Guide me to cultivate the qualities of honesty, loyalty, and compassion in my relationships, and to be a true friend to those who need it most. May your grace and love inspire me to be a source of light and encouragement to all those I encounter.
Amen.

111.

Prayer for Self-Control: Oh true God, source of all strength and discipline, I ask for your help in mastering my impulses and desires, and in

cultivating self-control and self-mastery. Help me to resist temptations that lead me away from my highest good, and to develop habits and practices that support my growth and development. May your grace and love empower me to live a life of self-mastery and inner freedom.
Amen.

112.

Prayer for Compassion: Oh true God, source of all compassion and love, I ask for your help in seeing the suffering of others and responding with kindness and generosity. Guide me to practice empathy and compassion towards all beings, and to work towards creating a world of justice and peace for all. May your grace and love inspire me to act with love and compassion towards all those I encounter.
Amen.

113.

Prayer for Healing: Oh true God, source of all healing and wholeness, I ask for your divine presence and guidance to bring healing to my body, mind, and spirit. Help me to take care of myself through good diet, exercise, and rest, and to seek out the wisdom of healers and physicians as needed. May your grace and love bring me comfort and strength as I journey towards wholeness.
Amen.

114.
Prayer for Gratitude: Oh true God, source of all blessings and abundance, I offer thanks for the gifts of life, love, and learning. Guide me towards practices of gratitude and appreciation, and help me to cultivate a heart of thankfulness. Let your grace and love flow through me, that I may be a source of joy and blessings to all those around me.
Amen.

115.
Oh true God, source of all sexuality and intimacy, Help me to embrace my sexuality with respect and dignity, and to treat others with love and compassion in all my relationships. Guide me towards practices that promote healthy sexuality, and help me to cultivate a deep and meaningful connection with my partner(s). Let your power flow through me, that I may experience the joys of intimacy with your grace and love, and that I may honor the divine spark within all beings.
Amen.

116.
Prayer for Self-Control:
Oh true God, source of all self-mastery and

discipline, Help me to control my impulses and desires, and to act with wisdom and restraint. Guide me towards practices that promote self-control and inner peace, and help me to cultivate a calm and centered mind. Let your power flow through me, that I may be a master of my own thoughts and emotions, and a source of inspiration to others.
Amen.

117.

Prayer for Defeating Evil:
Oh true God, beyond all forms and names, Help me to see through the illusions of this world, and to find the strength to overcome the darkness within and without. Guide me with your wisdom and protect me with your love, as I seek to defeat the forces of evil that threaten to consume me. Let your power flow through me, that I may be empowered to do your work in this world, and bring light to the darkness, that all may know your grace and love.
Amen.

118.

Prayer for Good Deeds:
Oh true God, source of all goodness and justice, Help me to be a force for good in this world, and to act with kindness, compassion, and justice towards others. Guide me towards deeds that promote well-being and happiness, and help me to make a positive difference in the lives of those around me. Let your

goodness flow through me, that I may be a bringer of light and hope to this world.
Amen.

119.

Prayer for Love:
Oh true God, source of all love and compassion, Help me to love others as I love myself, and to see the divinity in all living things. Guide me towards acts of kindness and generosity, and help me to cultivate a loving heart. Let your love flow through me, that I may be a vessel for your grace and compassion.
Amen.

120.

Prayer for Knowledge Seeking:
Oh true God, source of all knowledge and wisdom, Guide me towards truth and understanding, and help me to discern what is right and just. Grant me the courage to question my assumptions and beliefs, and to seek new insights and perspectives. Let your wisdom and understanding flow through me, that I may be a seeker of truth and a bringer of light to this world.
Amen.

121.

Prayer for Health:

Oh true God, source of all healing and strength, I ask for your grace and protection, that I may be healthy in body, mind, and spirit. Guide me towards practices that promote well-being, and help me to take care of myself and others. Let your healing power flow through me, that I may be a vessel for your love and compassion.
Amen.

122.

Prayer for Forgiveness:
Oh true God, source of all that is good and just, I confess my mistakes and failings, and ask for your forgiveness and grace. Help me to learn from my mistakes and grow in your light. Let your forgiveness flow through me, that I may forgive others as I have been forgiven, and be a source of healing and peace in this world.
Amen.

123.

Oh true God, source of compassion and mercy,
Help us to end the suffering of people and animals on this earth.
Guide us with your wisdom and grace, that we may create a world of peace and harmony for all beings.
Let your healing power flow through us,
that we may be a source of comfort and support to those who are in pain and in need of your grace.
Amen.

124.

Oh true God, beyond all forms and names,
Hear my prayer as I call upon your mercy and compassion.

I see the suffering of people and animals on this earth,
And it breaks my heart to witness such pain and injustice.

Help us to end the cycle of suffering and violence,
And to create a world of peace and harmony for all beings.

Guide us with your wisdom and grace,
That we may find the courage to stand up for what is right and just.

Help us to see the divinity in all living things,
And to treat them with the respect and kindness they deserve.

I offer myself up to you, true God, as a servant of your love and justice,
That I may work towards the liberation of all beings from suffering.

Let your healing power flow through me, that I may be a source of comfort and support,
To those who are in pain and in need of your grace.

Thank you for your love and compassion, which are always with us,

And for the hope and inspiration to create a better world for all beings.
Amen.

125.

Oh true God, source of all that is good and just,
I come before you with a heavy heart and a contrite spirit.

I confess my mistakes and failings, and ask for your forgiveness and grace,
That I may be cleansed of my sins and made whole once more.

Help me to see where I have gone wrong,
And to make amends where I have caused harm.

Guide me with your wisdom and compassion,
That I may learn from my mistakes and grow in your light.

I offer myself up to you, true God, as a vessel for your love and mercy,
That I may show compassion to others as you have shown to me.

Let your forgiveness flow through me, that I may forgive others as I have been forgiven,
And be a source of healing and peace in this world.

Thank you for your love and grace, which are always with me,
And for the opportunity to seek forgiveness and

renewal in your holy presence.

Amen.

126.

Oh true God, beyond all forms and names,
Hear my prayer, as I call upon your grace.

Help me to see through the illusions of this world,
And to find the strength to overcome the darkness within and without.

Guide me with your wisdom and protect me with your love,
As I seek to defeat the forces of evil that threaten to consume me.

Grant me the courage to face my fears and stand up for what is right,
Even when it is difficult, and to resist the temptations of the powers of darkness.

Surround me with your light and shield me from harm,
That I may be strengthened by your presence always.

I offer myself up to you, true God, as a vessel for your power,
That I may serve the greater good and be a beacon of hope to those around me.

Let your power flow through me, that I may be

empowered to do your work in this world,
And bring light to the darkness, that all may know your grace and love.

Amen.

127.

Oh true God, you who are beyond all forms and names, I call upon you now to be with me. Help me to see through the illusions of this world and to find the strength to overcome the darkness within and without. Guide me with your wisdom and protect me with your grace as I seek to defeat the forces of evil that threaten to consume me.

Grant me the courage to face my fears and to stand up for what is right, even when it is difficult. Help me to see through the deceptions of the powers of darkness and to resist their temptations. Protect me from harm and surround me with your love, that I may feel your presence always and be strengthened by it.

I offer myself up to you, true God, that you may work through me to defeat evil and bring light to this world. Use me as an instrument of your will, that I may serve the greater good and be a beacon of hope to those around me. Let your power flow through me, that I may be strengthened and empowered to do your work in this world.
Amen

128.

O Father of the Aeons, you who dwell in the highest realms of the spiritual world, we implore you to hear our plea. The demiurge and his archons seek to trap us in the cycle of birth and death, to bind us to this material realm and prevent us from attaining the true spiritual liberation that is our birthright.

Grant us the knowledge and the strength to break free from the shackles of the demiurge, to transcend the limitations of this world and ascend to the highest realms of spiritual well-being. Help us to cultivate our spiritual selves, to purify our souls of all that is impure and base, so that we may be worthy of entering into your divine presence.

May your divine light guide us on our journey, O Father of the Aeons, and help us to overcome the illusions and the deceptions of the archons. May we attain the highest possible state of spiritual well-being after we leave this world, and may we be reunited with our true spiritual selves in your presence.
Amen.

129.

O Divine Light, who shines forth from the depths of the unknown, we call upon you in our hour of need. The archons of the demiurge seek to distract us with the glittering baubles of this world, to lead us astray from the path of enlightenment and truth. But we know that true liberation can only be found in the spiritual realm, beyond the illusions of the material world.

Grant us the strength and the wisdom to reject the false promises of the archons, to turn away from the empty pleasures and the superficial distractions that they offer. Help us to cultivate our spiritual selves, to nurture the spark of divine light that resides within us. Guide us on the path of gnosis, that we may attain the knowledge of the mysteries and the wisdom that transcends all earthly knowledge.

May your divine light illuminate our minds and our hearts, O Divine Light, and lead us to the victory over the demiurge and his archons. We offer our souls and our spirits to you, that you may transform them into instruments of your divine will and purpose. Amen.

130.

O Father of Truth, who dwells in the depth of the unknowable, hear our plea for deliverance from the tyranny of the demiurge and his archons. You who are the source of all being, beyond the realm of the imperfect and the flawed, help us to awaken from the slumber of ignorance and to see through the illusions of this world.

Grant us the strength and courage to resist the temptations of the archons and to overcome their lies and deceit. Help us to remember our divine origin and to reclaim the spark of light that they have stolen from us. Guide us on the path of gnosis, that we may attain the knowledge of the mysteries and the wisdom that transcends all earthly knowledge.

May your light shine upon us, O Father of Truth, and lead us to the liberation of our souls from the bondage of the demiurge. We offer our hearts and our spirits to you, that you may transform them into vessels of your divine love and wisdom. Amen.

131.

O Father of the Aeons, you who exist beyond the limits of this false reality, we call out to you in desperation. Our souls are trapped in the snare of the archons, bound by the illusions of this world and the chains of the demiurge. We cry out to you for deliverance, for only you can break through the matrix and rescue us from this darkness.

We know that you are the source of all truth and light, the fount of all wisdom and knowledge. We beseech you to reveal to us the secrets of the divine, to lift the veil of ignorance that has been cast upon our minds. Show us the way to overcome the archons and to reclaim the spark of the divine that they have stolen from us.

We trust in your infinite mercy and compassion, O Father of the Aeons. We know that you will not abandon us to the clutches of the demiurge, but will come to our aid and lead us to the true freedom that can only be found in you. We offer our hearts and our souls to you, that you may transform them into vessels of your divine power and grace.
Amen.

132.

In the name of the Father and the Son and the Holy Spirit,
We invoke the divine spark within us,
The light of the Aeons that shines in the darkness,
Guiding us on our journey towards gnosis.
Through the power of the Sophia,
We transcend the illusions of this world,
And ascend to the realm of the Pleroma.
May the wisdom of the Logos illuminate our minds,
And the love of the Father embrace our hearts,
As we seek to know the mysteries of the divine.
Amen.

133.

I am a spark of the divine, a fragment of the eternal light. Through gnosis, I will transcend the material realm and unite with the source of all creation. As above, so below; as within, so without. By knowing myself, I will know the universe and the mysteries of the divine. Let the truth be revealed and the illusions of the demiurge be cast away. Amen.

134.

I am a spark of the divine, a fragment of the eternal light, and though I walk in darkness, I do not fear. Through gnosis, I know that this world of matter is but a fleeting illusion, and that my true home is in the realm of the divine. Let me trust in the wisdom of the aeons, and surrender my will to the guiding light of the Father. Let me remember that I am never alone, for the Holy Spirit is with me always, comforting and sustaining me in times of trial. And though I may face uncertainty and fear, I know that my soul is eternal, and that my ultimate destiny lies beyond the confines of this mortal existence. Amen.

135.

In the face of uncertainty and the mystery of death,
we turn to the divine spark within us,
the light that guides us on our journey.

As we grow old and face our mortality,
we seek comfort in the knowledge that we are not alone,
that the love of the divine sustains us.

In the face of loss and grief,
we trust in the transformative power of love,

that even in death, we are held in the embrace of the divine.

May we find strength in the wisdom of the ages,
and in the knowledge that we are part of a greater whole,
eternal beings on a journey of discovery and growth.

May we live each moment with intention and purpose,
and may our lives be a reflection of the divine spark within us,
a light that shines brightly even in the darkest of times.

Amen.

136.

Within me lies the spark of divine light,
A beacon of hope in times of plight.
Through turmoil and strife, I find my way,
With each breath, I am renewed today.

I cast aside all doubts and fears,
And in this moment, I am here.
With each exhale, I let go of stress,
And with each inhale, I find my peace and rest.

I am a child of the Divine,
With love and light that always shines.
Through every trial and every test,
I trust in the guidance that is my best.

So let my mind and heart be still,
And let my spirit be filled.
With every chant, I embrace my power,
To overcome all that would devour.

For I am strong, and I am free,
In this moment, I choose to be.
And with each chant, my soul takes flight,
Guided by the wisdom of eternal light.

Amen.

137.

From the light that shines within me, I radiate love and peace towards my neighbours, colleagues, and peers. I recognize that we are all reflections of the divine spark within us, and I seek to honour and nurture that spark in others as well as in myself. When confronted with negativity or conflict, I choose to respond with compassion and understanding, knowing that these are the tools of true spiritual growth. I release any attachment to anger or resentment and invite the wisdom of the divine to guide me towards a peaceful resolution. May the light of the divine within us all shine brightly and guide us towards unity and harmony. Amen.

138.

Oh divine spark within, guide us in our quest for liberation from this material world.
Lead us away from the traps of pride, envy, anger, and sloth,
Protect us from the pitfalls of gluttony, lust, and greed,
So that we may ascend to the light and merge with the eternal One.

May the wisdom of Sophia enlighten our minds,
And the love of Christ fill our hearts,
May we embrace the path of gnosis and attain the knowledge of the divine,
And in doing so, overcome the darkness within and without.

Oh, holy Pleroma, hear our prayer,
As we strive to overcome the seven deadly sins,
May our souls ascend to the heights of divine consciousness,
And find eternal peace in your embrace.
Amen.

139.

In the Name of the Divine Sophia, I release all attachments to the outcome of my desires. I surrender to the Divine Will, knowing that all is in Divine order. I trust in the guidance of the Divine Spark within me, and I know that rejection is merely an illusion of the material world. I choose to align with the higher truth of my spiritual essence and the infinite love of the Divine. Amen.

140.

I am a child of the Divine, and my worth is not defined by the words of others. I choose to focus on love, light, and truth, and release any negativity that comes my way. May all beings be free from the suffering caused by gossip, and may we all awaken to our true nature as beloved children of God. Amen.

141.

Oh, divine light within us all,
Shining bright, standing tall,
Through the darkness we must roam,
To find our way back home.

For hatred is a poison strong,
That taints our hearts and leads us wrong,
But love, the key to open doors,
Can heal our wounds and so much more.

Like a river flowing free,
Love can wash away our pain and debris,
And like a fire burning bright,
It can dispel the darkness of the night.

So let us not be swayed by hate,
But stand firm, unafraid and straight,
For we are all children of the divine,

And love will always be our guiding sign.

Let us extend our love and light,
To all who cross our path, day or night,
For in doing so, we can transform,
The world into a kinder, gentler norm.

Let love be our armor and shield,
In a world where hatred is revealed,
For in the end, it's love that will win,
And usher in a new age, free of sin.

Oh, divine light within us all,
Shining bright, standing tall,
Through the darkness we will roam,
With love as our compass, leading us home.

Amen.

142.

In the realm of the digital, let us seek the divine light.
May we use our screens to connect and uplift, not to deceive or fight.

Let us navigate these virtual waters with mindfulness and care,
For the world of the internet can be a dangerous snare.

May we remember the wisdom of the ancients and the teachings of Christ,
And use our social media presence to spread love,

truth, and light.

Let us not be seduced by the temptations of the online world,
But remain steadfast in our faith and in the truth we uphold.

May our posts and comments be filled with grace, kindness, and compassion,
And may we use our online presence to build bridges of connection and unity, not division.

Let us honor the sacredness of every being we encounter online,
And strive to be a force for good in this digital age, divine.

May this mantra remind us to use social media with intention and purpose,
And to always seek the guidance of the divine source.

Amen.

143.

May we see the divine spark in our family members, whether they be our children, parents, siblings, or extended kin. May we recognize that they, like us, are made in the image of the divine, and that their actions and behaviours are shaped by their own unique life experiences and circumstances.

May we approach our family members with

compassion and understanding, seeking to connect with them on a deeper level and to foster a sense of mutual respect and appreciation. May we recognize that our family relationships are sacred and that they offer us opportunities for growth, healing, and transformation.

May we release any feelings of anger, resentment, or judgment towards our family members, recognizing that these emotions only serve to create further separation and pain. Instead, may we cultivate a spirit of forgiveness and love, knowing that it is through these qualities that we can heal our relationships and create a more harmonious and loving family dynamic.

May we remember that we are all connected, that our actions and words have an impact on others, and that by choosing to approach our family members with love, we can create a ripple effect of positive change that extends far beyond our immediate family circle.

May we honour the divine within ourselves and within our family members, and may we continue to grow and evolve together in a spirit of love and unity.

Amen.

144.

May the light of the divine spark within me,

Illuminate the hearts of those who have wronged me.
May the wisdom of the Christ within me,
Guide me towards compassion and forgiveness.

May the love of the divine Sophia within me,
Heal the wounds caused by past grievances.
May the power of the Holy Spirit within me,
Transform all animosity into peace and harmony.

May the grace of the Father and the Mother above,
Embrace both friend and foe alike.
May the mercy of the Son and the Daughter below,
Redeem all souls from hatred and strife.

May all beings be blessed with understanding,
May all souls be united in the light.
May the truth of the aeons be revealed within us,
As we seek the divine within and without

Amen.

145.

Chanting mantra:
From the darkness of ignorance, lead me to the light of knowledge!

146.

Chanting mantra:
May the divine spark within me shine brightly!

147:
Chanting Mantra:
Guide me on the path of liberation from suffering.150

148:
Chanting Mantra:
May the light of the divine illuminate my relationships.

149:
Chanting Mantra:
Grant me the wisdom to see through illusion and recognize truth.

150:
May the light of the divine spark within me,
Illuminate the hearts of those who have wronged me.
May the wisdom of the Christ within me,
Guide me towards compassion and forgiveness.

May the love of the divine Sophia within me,
Heal the wounds caused by past grievances.
May the power of the Holy Spirit within me,
Transform all animosity into peace and harmony.

May the grace of the Father and the Mother above,
Embrace both friend and foe alike.

May the mercy of the Son and the Daughter below,
Redeem all souls from hatred and strife.

May all beings be blessed with understanding,
May all souls be united in the light.
May the truth of the aeons be revealed within us,
As we seek the divine within and without

Amen.

NOTES

NOTES

NOTES

NOTES

NOTES